FOR SELECTIVE SCHOOL TESTS, OPPORTUNITY CLASS TESTS AND PROBLEM SOLVING

BOOK 2

Mohan Dhall

Michael McKay, Creative Illustrator

Five Senses Education Pty Ltd
2/195 Prospect Highway
Seven Hills 2147
New South Wales
Australia

First Published 2021

Dhall, Mohan
Critical Thinking Skills – Book 2

ISBN 978-1-76032-407-0

Contents

Foreword

Critical thinking is an essential skill that students need to develop. Critical thinking is evidenced when students can analyse data, evaluate options and alternatives and critique information for its coherence. It also is evidenced when students ask meaningful questions, can hypothesise, and also explain reasons to account for observed relationships and patterns. Students who can generalise from the specific and can then appraise their generalisations, and who can propose and justify solutions to complex problems, demonstrate critical thinking skills.

In a rapidly changing world, characterised by multiple and competing information sources, developing critical thinking skills and the ability to reason logically has never been more important. Critical thinking is a fundamental skill for a meaningful life.

Practice on the problems in this book will help students to develop a range of critical thinking skills. Prior to practising, students should read through the section at the start which provides strategies. Using these strategies will be helpful to developing the skills required to think through complex problems.

The author would like to acknowledge Michael McKay the creative illustrator who assisted with editing, made helpful suggestions and whose graphic work can be seen throughout in the 2D and 3D puzzles.

About the author

Mohan Dhall is an experienced teacher and teacher-educator, author and educational manager. Trained in gifted education, Mohan has developed many critical thinking courses for students and has also trained teachers in critical and creative thinking skills. As Director, he ran one of Australia's longest running school-based centres for gifted children. He has written hundreds of different types of critical thinking questions and had more than 70 books published. Mohan is currently the Academic Leader of M2K Education and Advisory.

Critical Thinking - An Introduction

Critical thinking involves the application and the development of a number of different thinking skills. Aspects of critical thinking include skills involving each of the following:

- Analysing
- Interpreting
- Evaluating
- Explaining
- Justifying
- Sequencing
- Reasoning – deductive and inductive
- Comparing
- Questioning
- Critiquing
- Inferring
- Hypothesising
- Appraising
- Assessing
- Testing
- Generalising
- Extrapolating and interpolating

At the core of many of these thinking skills is logic. Logic is an application of the principles of reasoning to evidence or data. Two important aspects of logical reasoning are deductive reasoning and inductive reasoning.

Deductive reasoning

This type of thinking requires a person to be able to draw valid or certain conclusions from a premise or premises as well as the application of defined rules.

Inductive reasoning

This type of thinking requires a person to be able to draw general conclusions from the premises which may not be certain. The generalisation should be plausible, but there will not be certainty.

Students may find that they are distracted by generalisations that are plausible but are not assured. It is essential that students ask themselves, "Is this answer certain?" before they make a choice.

Examples of different reasoning skills

Examples demonstrating different aspects of each of these types of thinking are shown in the pages that follow.

Deductive reasoning

This type of thinking requires a person to be able to draw valid or certain conclusions from a premise or premises as well as the application of defined rules.

Logical application of rules

Rules guide actions. This means that following rules will be a guide as to what has to be done in a given situation. Rules are situation specific because they vary depending on the activity. For example, the offside rule in soccer does not apply in another sporting code like Australian Rules Football (AFL). Similarly, the driving rules vary between countries, from something as simple as which side of the road people drive on.

Logical reasoning

Logical reasoning tests thinking through the application of logic. Logic requires the application of rules. Using logical reasoning may require successive applications or several steps be taken.

When solving logical reasoning problems, start with asking, "What do we know?"

That is, is there data and rules given that need to be considered? If so, having a clear mind and holding what is important in working memory will help. If unsure, highlight or write down the key data and the rules that need to be applied.

Also, keep a clear mind on what the problem is that needs to be solved.

Application of rules

Where rules are given follow them. Apply each one, reading it carefully. When there are multiple steps, this can be complicated so it can be useful to read each one out loud so it can be heard. This assists with retention through using auditory working memory.

When doing questions with rules or where there is a definition, those rules or that definition must be applied consistently.

Deduction - Arrangements

Deduction is applied when arranging items in order according to pre-defined rules that indicate where they should be. Arranging items in order, or matching data according to rules, can also take the form of applying rules across data sets when the data sets overlap. This is shown in the question below.

Arrangements – an Example

In a recipe there are eight different herbs to choose from: rosemary, thyme, parsley, sage, oregano, marjoram, cilantro and basil.

The chef cannot use any more than five ingredients for an acceptable recipe. The rules for use of the ingredients are as follows:

- Thyme cannot be used with parsley or marjoram
- Marjoram is often used with sage
- Sage must be used with oregano
- Basil cannot be used with either cilantro or oregano
- Sage must be used with cilantro

Which of the following groups of herbs would be acceptable in a recipe?

A Thyme, basil, cilantro, marjoram and oregano

B Oregano, cilantro, thyme, sage and rosemary

C Marjoram, parsley, cilantro, basil and sage

D Basil, rosemary, parsley, cilantro and thyme

Solution

Here there is a series of rules that need to be applied. Firstly, none of the answers has more than 5 ingredients so this rule is satisfied. Secondly, as thyme cannot be with parsley or marjoram, A can be ruled incorrect. This also eliminates D. Thirdly, Sage must be used with oregano, hence B is fine, but C is not. C is also eliminated by the next rule: "basil cannot be used with either cilantro or oregano". Hence B is correct.

Deduction - Syllogism

A syllogism is a type of logical reasoning where a conclusion needs to be validly drawn from two or more given premises. A premise is a given rule: a fact, statement or truth. Whilst the rule may not be literally true, for the purposes of the exercise and the application of rules, the premise is generally held to be true. An example is shown below.

Syllogism – an Example

All building blocks are made of sandstone.

All sandstones contain quartz.

If these bold statements are true what can be correctly concluded?

A Everything containing quartz can be used for making building blocks

B If something contains quartz it must be sandstone

C All building blocks contain quartz

D All sandstones make building blocks

Solution

The answer is as follows. A is incorrect on account of a misapplication of inductive reasoning. Inductive reasoning occurs where a generalisation is made from specific events. This misapplication of logical reasoning afflicts B as well. D we cannot be certain of as the premise is building blocks are made of sandstone, not all sandstones make building blocks. It is possible that some forms of sandstone are not able to be made into building blocks.

C is correct as if all sandstones are made of quartz and all building blocks are made of sandstone, then all building blocks, being made of sandstone, must also contain quartz.

Inductive reasoning

This type of thinking requires a person to be able to draw general conclusions from the premises which may not be certain. The generalisation should be plausible, but there will not be certainty.

Students may find that they are distracted by generalisations that are plausible but are not assured. It is essential that students ask themselves, "Is this answer certain?" before they make a choice.

Generalised statements from particular data sets

This type of reasoning looks at data or trends and then makes generalised statements based on this. Consider the following:

- Reynard scored highest on the first test in January 2018 and won the prize at the end of that year.
- Reynard did not score highest on the first test in January 2019 and did not win the prize at the end of that year.
- Reynard scored highest on the first test in January 2020 and won the prize again at the end of that year.
- Reynard scored highest on the first test in January 2021. He should win the prize at the end of the year.

The final point made here is a conclusion based on the prior evidence. It may or may not hold true.

This process follows the application of inductive reasoning skills.

Strategies for dealing with logical fallacies

A fallacy is an error or mistake in the logical thinking process. A fallacy can arise for a number of reasons. Such reasons include mistake (error) and "*all or nothing*" thinking (such as, "if it is not white it must be black").

An example of a fallacy in operation can be seen as follows:

> *"Denly is often wrong about the weather. He says tomorrow it will rain. So, it will not rain tomorrow."*

The problem here is the conflation of 'often' with 'always'. It is not at all definite that Denly is wrong on ***all*** occasions. After all, he is 'often wrong' not 'always' wrong. Moreover, a prediction can prove to be incorrect. Hence it is certainly possible that it may rain tomorrow.

Another form of this fallacy makes the incorrect assumption that just because something has been, then it must always be. An example can be seen here:

> *"I can see why we have a minimum wage. People need a minimum amount of income to live. But you cannot have a limit on how much people earn. It has never worked like that. It will stop people being ambitious. So, we can never even consider the idea of a maximum wage."*

There are several logical errors here:

1. The error that something cannot be considered because it has not previously been used as a solution to an issue.
2. The error that you cannot limit how much people earn. Taxes reduce how much people earn and salary caps in sport limit how much people earn. Hence, the notion "it has never worked before" is erroneous, as evidently it has worked and continues to work.
3. The assumption that a limit is appropriate at one end (low incomes) but not at another end (very high incomes).

Types of fallacy

There are different types of logical error that are quite commonly seen. These include each of the following:

- The "excluded middle" fallacy
- False attribution
- The Bandwagon fallacy

Each of these can come up during an argument.

The "excluded middle" fallacy

Here the logical error takes different forms, both based on a failure of inductive reasoning. One form is applying only the extremes, such as all or nothing. Examples are, "*If you are not with me, you are against me*" or "*If it is not white, it must be black.*" Here the range of in between or middle choices is not considered. If something is not white it may be at least ten thousand other colours or shades of other colours. It does not have to be black. Similarly, "*If you are not with me*" you might not be interested in me. You might not know me. You might be with someone else. You might also be against me. Clearly, there are host of other alternatives rather than the simplified binary choices given.

A second form is when a small amount of something is posed as good, then more of it is assumed to be better. Or, if a small amount of something is bad then more is worse. Consider these examples:

> *"If you eat salad, it is healthy. So, we should eat only salad always as it will be healthier."*
>
> *"It hurts if I exercise. Hence, I should not exercise. If I do more exercise, it will hurt more."*

Further logical errors arise when there is false attribution. This is detailed below.

False attribution

Consider the following statements:

> *Speeding is illegal. There is an increased incidence of accidents when people speed. Yesterday I saw a man speeding, and later I saw he crashed. This proves that speeding causes accidents.*

The issue here is that we do not know why the car crashed or even whether, at the time of the crash, the driver was speeding. It could be that the driver was NOT speeding but was distracted. It could be that another driver was responsible for the crash. It could be that there was a mechanical failure with the car, or that the driver had a medical episode and was unable to control the vehicle. There are numerous alternative and also plausible possibilities.

Hence, attributing the crash to one possibility only, when the others have not been ruled out, is an attribution error. This means that something is being attributed (speeding) when it may not be the cause.

False attribution often happens when there is coincidence. This can be seen as follows:

> *"I ate an apple and then I felt sick. The apple must have caused me to be sick."*

The issue here is that feeling sick occurred immediately after eating an apple. However, the cause of feeling sick has not been determined. Hence to attribute the sickness to eating the apple is false attribution, unless it is certain and factual that the apple was the cause of the sickness.

If every other possible cause of sickness is tested and ruled out then the apple may have been the cause of the sickness, but without ruling out other possibilities there is no certainty of a ***causal link*** between the two events.

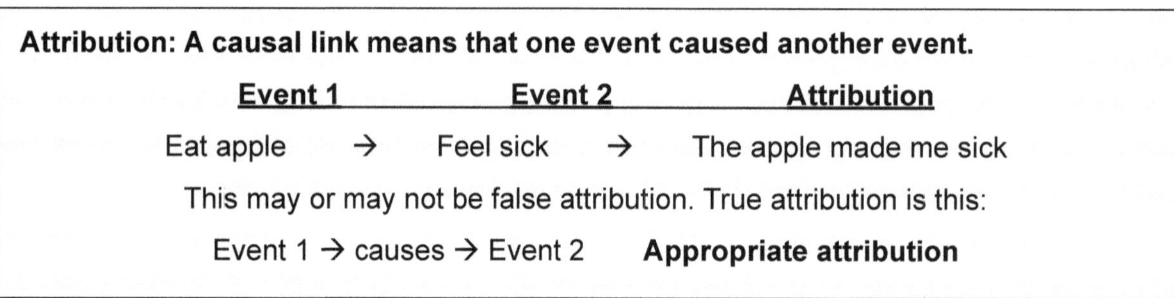

Attribution: A causal link means that one event caused another event.

Event 1		Event 2		Attribution
Eat apple	→	Feel sick	→	The apple made me sick

This may or may not be false attribution. True attribution is this:

Event 1 → causes → Event 2 **Appropriate attribution**

A further example of false attribution can be seen in these statements:

> *"Donny was tired today because he didn't sleep well. This explains why he dropped the rugby ball so many times."*

Firstly, we do not know whether Donny is tired because he did not sleep well or from some other factor. Secondly, tired people may or may not drop rugby balls. The reason for Donny dropping the ball is attributed to the fact that he was tired – but it also may not be true at all. However, Donny may have dropped the ball because he had no skill or because he was not looking at it.

Hence it can be seen that there is false attribution.

Arguments

An argument is a cohesive set of reasons given in support of a position. Argument is strong when the position is clear. Argument is also strong when the reasons cited to strengthen the argument are supported by facts or evidence that is unbiased. This means that opinion does not strengthen argument but actually weakens it.

Students are to understand how to critique an argument. An argument requires a logical and cohesive structure and that evidence be used to support the argument. You need to understand that argument is weakened by each of the following:

- Irrelevant statements
- Hearsay
- Opinion

Irrelevant means that it is not related to the substance of what is being argued. Hearsay means that it is information which is indirect and cannot be verified. Usually hearsay takes the form of, "*someone said to me that...*" Opinion is an uninformed or subjective view of something, unless that opinion is expert opinion, which is informed and is more objective (based on independent, factual evidence).

If you see these elements in a person's argument, then they do not add strength to the argument. The exception to these rules applies to opinion. If the person who is giving the opinion is a recognised 'authority' or specialist, then their expert opinion may strengthen an argument. So, always ask, "Who is giving the opinion and in what capacity are they giving it?"

When assessing an argument, you need to ask crucial questions:

- What EXACTLY is being argued?
- What will strengthen the argument?
- What will weaken the argument?

These questions form the basis of analysis for these types of questions.

The slippery slope argument

Here the fallacy is that if one thing is done then it will inevitably lead to other things occurring which are very bad. An example is this,

> *"If a government decriminalises drugs, then everybody will take drugs."*

This is clearly not the case as has been shown in numerous countries around the world

Argument and the Bandwagon Fallacy

Here the person making the argument seeks to strengthen their argument through appealing to what 'everyone thinks', 'everyone knows' or 'should be obvious as most people know it.'

The issue here is that it is not true. Sometimes statistics are also used to make it seem as though there is factual strength based on data.

Consider the following: Felicity surveys fifteen people to ask them their favourite colour. The answers are:

- 8 people say blue
- 1 says green,
- 2 say purple,
- 1 says red
- 2 say black
- 1 says pink.

Felicity then states, "*most people say blue is their favourite colour*".

There are two issues here: the small sample size (the small number of people surveyed) and the use of the term "most" which implies most out of ALL people.

Argument and the "excluded middle"

The excluded middle is a logical error that only looks at the extremes. For example, a statement that asserts if something is not hot it must be cold. However, if it is not hot – it could be warm. It could be very, very hot. It could be frozen (extremely cold).

The excluded middle occurs when inductive reasoning is misapplied.

False dichotomies

Here students are presented with events that seem to be exclusive (do not overlap) but actually they do overlap. Consider this:

All dogs have four legs. Cats have four legs. Therefore, cats are dogs.

What is wrong with the logic here?

Here there is an assumption made that since all dogs have four legs then the 'reverse case' is also true. Here we are looking at a subset of a set: within the set of ALL creatures that have four legs, is the set called 'dogs'.

There is a false dichotomy set up. This means that two scenarios have been created in such a way as to give seemingly opposing sets of information. This is a failure in the application of inductive reasoning.

A false dichotomy is a logical fallacy, or a failure of logical reasoning. It occurs when a person is presented with a limited number of options which are presented as the ***only options available***.

An example is captured in this quote by former US President Bush: *"If you are not with us, you are against us."*

False dichotomies arise from misunderstanding. They can be used by people to deliberately mislead, oversimplify or obfuscate the full range of options available. Politicians can use false dichotomies in a way so as to pressure people or make opposing politicians appear to support a stance that they do not support.

Another example of a false dichotomy is this: *"if you do not let me search you then you must be guilty."*

An extension of false dichotomies if false attribution discussed earlier. This can occur when people conflate coincidence with causation. This can happen for example if a person feels cold and then later has a sore throat. It is common for this coincidence to be characterised as: *"because you were cold you are now sick."*

Analogy and false analogy

An analogy involves comparing one thing with another thing with a view to explaining the second thing. For example, trunk is to tree as tyre is to car. Another example is this:

Scale : Weight as Ammeter : Current

False analogy occurs when the comparison made is made incorrectly so that a false or wrong conclusion is drawn.

Consider this: *"A footballer's body is a battering ram, so they have to learn to keep playing after getting knocked down."*

Concussion is a highly dangerous brain injury that occurs from heavy head knocks. The comparison with a battering ram acts to minimise the dangerous effects of heavy impacts to the human body.

Hypothesis testing

Logical reasoning tests thinking through the application of logic. An hypothesis is an attempt to understand or explain something that is observed. However, the explanation is untested and becomes the starting point for further testing or investigation.

Consider the following

> *Dungri notices that every time it is sunny the black dog next door lies in the sun. Dungri creates a hypothesis that the dog likes warmth.*

This is, however, untested. It seems to explain the dog's behaviour, but it could be an incorrect explanation.

It is possible that the dog likes light. It could be possible that the dog feels cramped inside and it is coincidental that it goes outside as the front door is open on sunny days.

Scientific reasoning and hypothesis testing

Scientific reasoning is logical reasoning applied to scientific data. That is, factual, observable, measurable data. Using data, scientists posit reasons for the observed data sets. The reasons seek to explain why the data shows the trends it does.

Hypothesis testing is important to critical thinking and scientific reasoning. Consider the following example.

Scientific reasoning and hypothesis testing – an example

Facts

1. Reptiles have four legs. They are tetrapods.
2. Reptiles are amniotes. This means that if their young are born from eggs, within the eggs will be an elastic sac.
3. Reptiles are vertebrates. This means that they have a backbone.
4. Reptiles are cold blooded. That is, their body temperature is dependent on the outside (environmental) temperature.
5. Reptiles breathe air through lungs.
6. Reptiles have scales.

Additional facts

1. Most amphibians have four legs.
2. Amphibians are cold blooded.
3. Amphibians lay their eggs in water and must live close to water.
4. Amphibians are vertebrates. This means they have a backbone.
5. Amphibians breathe through lungs.
6. Amphibians have smooth skins.

Based on this, which of the following is **not correct**?

A It can be hypothesised that if an animal is a vertebrate, it could be a reptile or an amphibian

B It can be hypothesised that if an animal breathes through lungs, it could be an amphibian

C It can be hypothesised that if an animal has four legs it will be a reptile but may not be an amphibian

D It can be hypothesised that if an animal has smooth skin and lives near water, it may be an amphibian

Solution

A can be logically concluded for two reasons. (1) Reptiles have four legs as most amphibians do so within all of the animals that have 4 legs, there are reptiles and most amphibians. (2) The word "could" is used. This means it is possible, not definitive.

B can also be logically concluded as, since amphibians breathe through lungs, within the group of all animals that breathe through lungs there will be amphibians.

D can be logically concluded as amphibians live close to water and have smooth skins. Hence within the range of animals that have smooth skins and live near water, amphibians are included. Also note the use of the words "may be".

C is **incorrect** as within the range of animals that have 4 legs, reptiles are a subset. Hence, it does not follow that if an animal has 4 legs it must be a reptile. The distractor here is the purported comparison to amphibians, most of which have 4 legs.

Estimation

Logical reasoning can be applied to a process of estimation. Estimation can involve making educated guesses. An 'educated' guess, is not an unconsidered guess. "Educated' means that a process of logical reasoning has been followed.

Estimation can also involve extrapolation or interpolation as methods of estimating.

Extrapolation means to apply the rule or trend given, or from a different situation, to a current problem.

Interpolation has two different applications in logical reasoning. The first is to use a method of inductive logic to find missing data. The second is to remove data which has been placed as a distractor and is not relevant. Either of these forms of inductive reasoning can be assessed.

Non-mutually exclusive events

Mutually exclusive means that events are independent and do not overlap. Non-mutually exclusive means that the events, situations or data do overlap. An example is this: There are 15 children. 12 of the children wear blue shorts. 8 of the children wear green T-shirts. Given the data we know that a child or children must wear both shorts and T-shirts. But how many?

Here the data is presented is such a way as to imply there are more than 15 children, since 12 and 8 is 20 – not 15. However, the data overlaps, meaning the sets are not exclusive.

This is shown in a Venn Diagram below. Here let A be the number of the children wearing blue shorts (AND NOT a green t-shirt). Let B represent the number wearing both. And let C equal the number of students wearing a green t-shirt but NOT blue shorts.

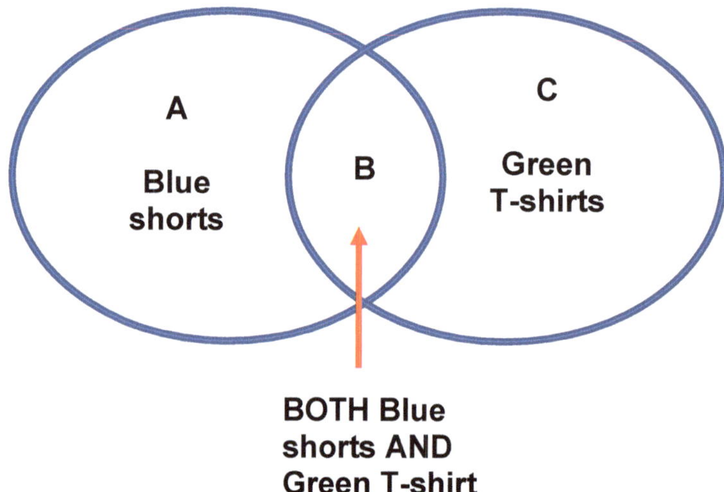

We know that: A + B = 12. We also know that B + C = 8. Finally, A + B + C = 15.

So, A must be 7, B = 5 and C = 3.

Picture completion problems

Picture completion requires a capacity to understand visual information, see patterns and pay attention to detail when presented with visual information. In the example below there is a pattern on a carpet Look closely at how the symbols turn or flip.

Spatial relationships - 2D shapes

The spatial relationship found in two-dimensional shapes can require a student to notice symbol rotations or other iterative changes between successive shapes. However, it can also require looking at two alternating patterns.

Spatial relationships - 3D shapes

Here there are questions that may require rotation or 'viewing' from multiple angles. This can be a tricky skill. Consider the following shape.

How many yellow blocks are there? 12 are visible. Some people will say 13 are visible – but are we viewing the ***side*** of the back cube ***or the top of one beside it***? Are there 35 – with the only missing block being in the corner?

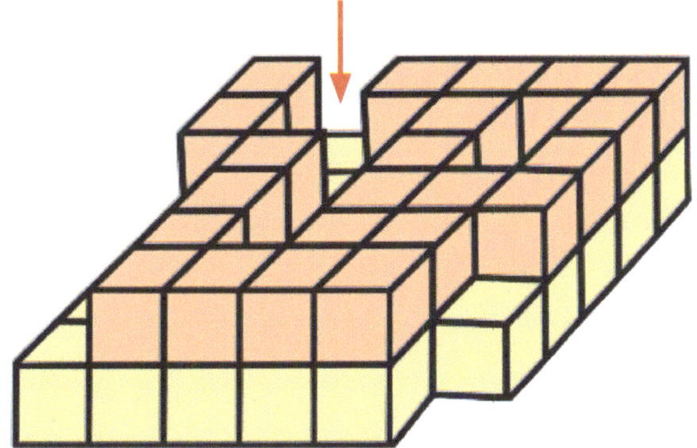

Is there a yellow block UNDER each of the orange blocks or not? Here we can see that 3D shapes can give information which leads the viewer to make assumptions. Those assumptions needed to be tested.

In this way, viewers can learn to assess and critique visual data.

Test timing

When preparing for tests the issue of time arises. This means, the issue of how to manage doing the questions, and getting as many correct as possible, in the limited time given.

As a general rule, **students should not worry** about time while they are learning ***how*** to solve the different types of questions. They need to focus on what to do first. They then need to practise questions repeatedly until they build their confidence and understand how to apply a range of strategies.

Once the range of questions is understood and different approaches known, then **the last thing** to practise is time management.

This will involve revisiting all practice questions, but out of order, and working to a pre-set time. This time should be the same as the actual test time. The aim is to see how many questions can be completed when pressured by time.

Since students will know how to solve the questions, they do not need to worry that they "can't". Simply, students need to remind themselves to stay focused and just work as quickly as they can without allowing themselves to get flustered or anxious.

Critical Thinking Problems

Question 1

The diagram below shows some aircraft around an airport. A bearing of 0° is North. The rules regarding landing are as follows:

Rule 1: Emergency vehicles land first

Rule 2: Planes with two engines land after planes with four engines

Rule 3: Planes arriving from the South East are preparing to land

Rule 4: Planes with four engines are international flights. Planes with two engines are domestic flights

Rule 5: White helicopters are used by the ambulance corps

Rule 6: Light aircraft land after helicopters. Helicopters are given the second lowest priority for landing

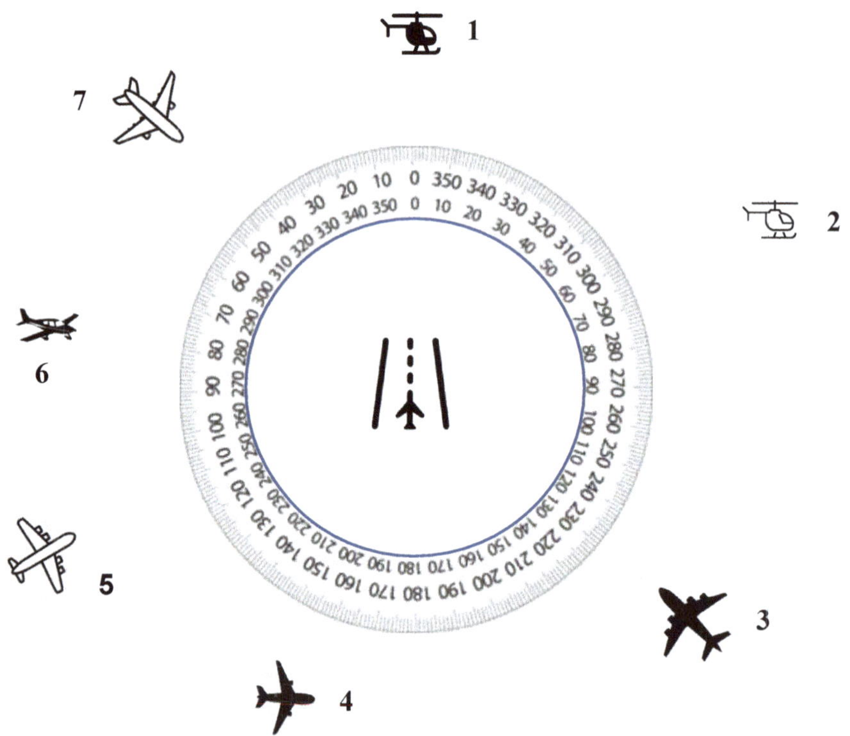

Which of the aircraft will land fourth and which will land sixth respectively?

A Aircraft 4 and Aircraft 1 respectively

B Aircraft 7 and Aircraft 6 respectively

C Aircraft 7 and Aircraft 1 respectively

D Aircraft 4 and Aircraft 6 respectively

Question 2

Souraya states, "Mark is independent and likes to do new things. He once decided to ride a bike up a hill because he wanted to see what his town looked like from a height. On another occasion Mark slept in a tent outside because he wanted to test if it was possible to see at night, when it is dark. His mother told him that there were other ways to find out. His uncle said that in some places it is so dark at night you cannot see your hand if you hold it out in front of you."

Which one of these statements, if true, is best **strengthens** Souraya's argument?

A Mark's teacher generally lets Mark do what he wants

B Mark tried to create a fishing net from wool to catch yabbies

C According to scientific studies, many young people like to try new things

D Mark once hurt himself when he fell from a tree in a park that had a sign saying, "*Do not climb*".

Question 3

Brenda says, "Wood can be harder than steel. In some places of the world, wood is used to build very large structures. The wood is so strong that steel-toothed saws cannot cut it or even mark the wood. These structures can be temples and other places of worship or remembrance, community halls and schools. Many such structures are over one-thousand-years old and even insects cannot bore into the wood. The Green Society says that wood is recyclable, and it is best used in all buildings."

Which one of these statements, if true, most **strengthens** Brenda's argument?

A Wood can be used to build structures that are over five storeys tall

B The Tasmanian Wood Society released a statement to the media saying that wood should be used in all buildings instead of steel or aluminium

C Steel can be tempered to make it stronger, and this steel is used in sawmills

D Steel nails cannot be hammered into hardwood trees

Use the following information to answers Questions 4, 5, 6 and 7.

Tom, Sandy, Daniel and Kuong have 40 lollies each.

They take it in turns to flip a $2-coin, $1-coin, a 50-cent piece and a 20-cent piece

The rules of their game are:

- If the $2-coin lands on heads that player has to give each of the others 5 lollies
- If the $2-coin lands on tails that player receives 3 lollies from each of the other players
- If the $1-coin lands on heads that player has to give each of the others 4 lollies
- If the $1-coin lands on tails that player receives 3 lollies from each of the other players
- If the 50-cent coin lands on heads that player has to give each of the others 3 lollies
- If the 50-cent coin lands on tails that player receives 4 lollies from each of the other players
- If the 20-cent coin lands on heads that player has to give each of the others 3 lollies
- If the 20-cent lands on tails that player receives 5 lollies from each of the other players

In order, Tom flips the $2-coin, Sandy the $1-coin, Daniel the 50-cent coin and Kuong the 20-cent coin.

The coins land, in order, as follows:

Head, Tail, Head, Head

Question 4

How many lollies does each player have after the third coin lands but before the fourth coin is tossed?

A Tom: 25 Sandy: 57 Daniel: 42 Kuong: 36

B Tom: 45 Sandy: 54 Daniel: 33 Kuong: 45

C Tom: 25 Sandy: 57 Daniel: 33 Kuong: 45

D Tom: 28 Sandy: 45 Daniel: 45 Kuong: 36

Question 5

After one full set of coin tosses the players have this number of lollies:

Tom: 44 lollies **Sandy 44 lollies** **Daniel 20 lollies** **Kuong 52 lollies**

What side did the coins land on?

A Tom: Tail, Sandy: Head, Daniel: Head, Kuong: Tail

B Tom: Head, Sandy: Head, Daniel: Head, Kuong: Head

C Tom: Tail, Sandy: Tail, Daniel: Head, Kuong: Tail

D Tom: Tail, Sandy: Tail, Daniel: Head, Kuong: Head

Question 6

After each person has tossed their coins, it goes back to Tom and they all toss again and **again in the same order. Again, each person starts with 40 lollies.**

If the coin tosses are: H, T, H, T, H, T, H, H, T, T, H, T, T, T then which person is the first to have no lollies left?

A Tom

B Sandy

C Daniel

D Kuong

Question 7

The players decide to alter the rules so the amount they give or receive is doubled. **They toss again in the same order, Tom, then Sandy, then Daniel and Kuong.**

Who has 24 lollies after this pattern of coin throws? T T H T H H T H

A Tom

B Sandy

C Daniel

D Kuong

Use this information to do Questions 8, 9 and 10.

The colours of the rainbow in order are:

Red, Orange, Yellow, Green, Blue, Indigo and Violet.

Jenny has a basket of pegs that are coloured with these same colours. She calls green the "neutral" colour as it is in the middle. When she hangs clothes on the clothesline she tries to balance the colours so that they "add" to Green. For example, if she uses a Blue peg, she will match it with a Yellow peg ***on the same item*** of clothing. Across the whole set of hung clothes Jenny wants the balance of colours to be neutral. An example is shown below.

Jenny hangs her clothes as shown below:

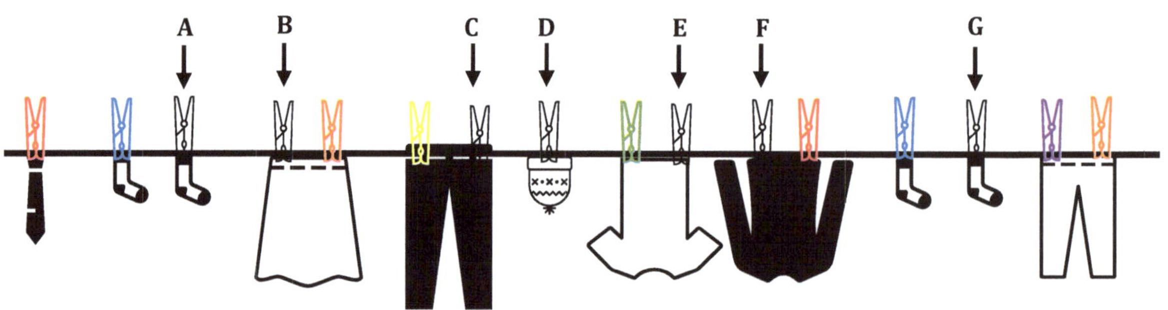

Question 8

In order, what colours should pegs A, B, C, D, E, F and G be?

A Yellow, Indigo, Blue, Violet, Green, Indigo, Yellow

B Yellow, Indigo, Blue, Violet, Green, Violet, Yellow

C Red, Indigo, Blue, Violet, Green, Violet, Yellow

D Yellow, Indigo, Blue, Green, Green, Violet, Yellow

Question 9

Jenny numbers the pegs from 1 to 7 in order, with Red = 1, Orange = 2 etc...

She stores the pegs in a box as shown. The value of each coloured peg is denoted by a symbol as shown in the box.

Which of these does NOT represent collections of pegs of equal value?

A 7 or 4 or [3 + 6]

B 5 or [2 + 5] or [3 + 4]

C [6 +] or 3 or [2 + 4]

D [8 +] or [7 + 2.5] or [4 +]

Question 10

Which of the following represents the number 7,734,145,672,156?

A V,VGY,RGB,IVO,RBV

B V,VYB,RBG,IVO,RVI

C V,VYG,RGB,IVO,RVI

D V,VYG,RGB,IVO,RBI

Use the following to answer Questions 11 and 12.

The times below were recorded for a runner training for a 15 km race. This is a diary that covers five consecutive weeks of training.

The times recorded are in minutes and seconds. This means 31:26 is read as 31 minutes and 26 seconds.

	Mon	Tues	Wed	Thurs	Fri	Sat	Sun
Week 1							
Run length	6 km	4 km	4 km	REST	4 km	REST	12 km
Time	31:26	19:09	18:53	-	18:48	-	70:00
Week 2							
Run length	6 km	4 km	REST	REST	4 km	REST	14 km
Time	32:00	19.02	-	-	18:21	-	80:00
Week 3							
Run length	6 km	4 km	REST	4 km	4 km	REST	16 km
Time	32:30	18:58	-	18:25	18:11	-	90:00
Week 4							
Run length	6 km	4 km	REST	4 km	4 km	REST	12 km
Time	33:30	18:23	-	18:07	17:55	-	59:20
Week 5							
Run length	6 km	4 km	4 km	REST	4 km	REST	14 km
Time	31:23	19:07	18:55	-	18:42	-	81:00

Question 11

What **cannot** be **hypothesised** from the data presented?

A Running times on Mondays are slower per kilometre due to the Sunday long run

B As Sunday runs get longer the fastest 4 km times in the followin week get lower

C 4 km runs on Tuesday are slowest because of the previous days of running

D A fourth 4 km run on Saturdays will be faster than the 4 km runs on Fridays

Question 12

The data for week 6 is presented below.

Week 6							
Run length	6 km	4 km	4 km	REST	4 km	REST	14 km
Time	32:20	18:56	18.39	-	?	-	80:21

Which of these correctly **predicts and justifies** the 4 km running time on Friday?

A 18 minutes and 20 seconds as it looks like Week 3 being repeated

B 18 minutes and 35 seconds as there has been only 1 rest day after 3 running days

C 18 minutes and 37 seconds as it is similar to Week 1

D 18 minutes and 18 seconds as the Week 5 Sunday run was 14 km

Question 13

Which of the following is the missing shape?

A

B

C

D

Question 14

It is known that one side effect of a vaccine is blood clotting. It is known that this side effect is rare. It is also known that people under 50 are most at risk and females are at greater risk than males. The blood clotting disorder is known in medicine and occurs naturally—but is very uncommon.

A 34-year-old woman and a 34-year-old man were given the vaccine. Afterwards the woman developed blood clots. She had never had any blood clots prior to taking the vaccine.

Which of the following is true?

A The vaccine caused the blood clot

B The vaccine probably caused the blood clot

C The vaccine may have caused the blood clot

D The vaccine cannot have caused the blood clot

Question 15

Look closely at the cube on the left below and its net to the right.

If you were to view this cube from underneath what would the face look like?

A

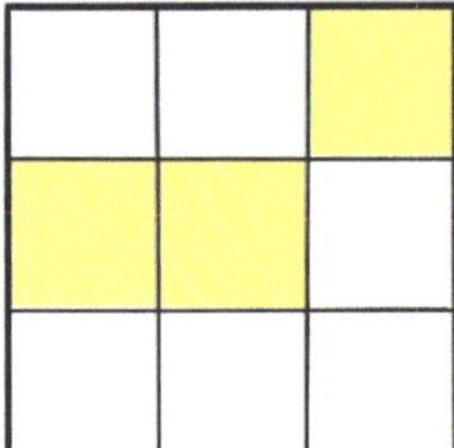

B

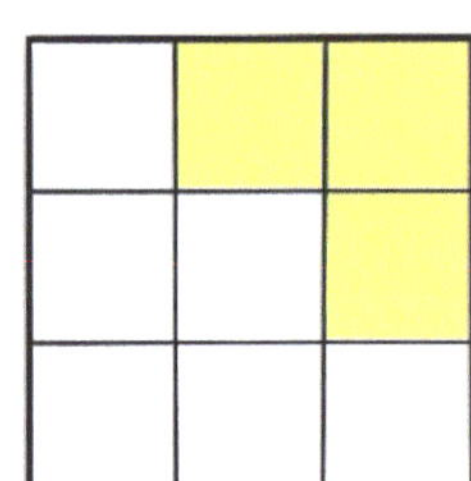

C

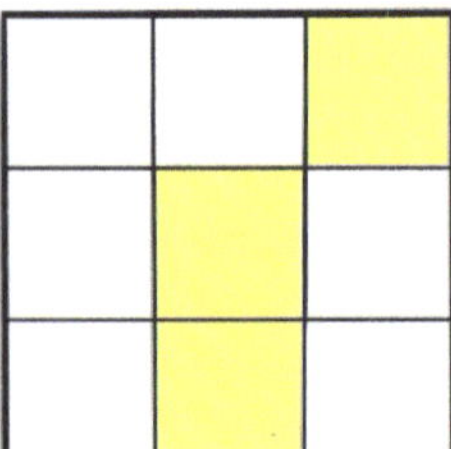

D

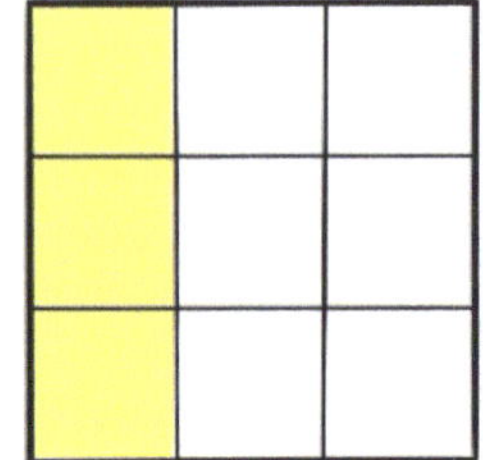

Use this information for Question 16 and 17.

The following are rules that maximise the strength of passwords used for access to online information:

- At least eight characters in length
- Are hard to guess
- Contain a variety of characters, numbers and special symbols
- Should contain at least three out of four of: Upper case letter(s), lowercase letter(s), digits and symbols
- Do not use consecutive characters
- Do not use predictable keyboard or numerical arrangements like "12345678" or or "Qwerty7*"
- Should not be obvious words like: "Password123"
- Should not repeat passwords again and again with slight variations
- Numbers substituting letters are stronger that just letters making words

Question 16

Which of the following is the **strongest** password?

A Dd12*!76

B uV%3m(2P

C #5Ms1)pV

D $^91vY43

Question 17

Jason has been using this password for his bank account: JasoN12#$

His partner's name is Sally. His cat's name is Seefah and his middle name is Bertram. Jason's bank tells him it is time to change his password.

Possible passwords				
jA50n23$%	Sally42@*	jASoN123#	B3rtR4M!2	533fJ@h2

In order, which of the following first listed passwords is the **weakest** new password and which of the second listed new passwords is the **strongest**?

A jA50n23$% and 533fJ@h2

B jASoN123# and B3rtR4M!2

C Sally42@* and jA50n23$%

D B3rtR4M!2 and jASoN123#

Question 18

You can have economic growth without economic development. Economic growth is a reference to the total output of goods and services created by a nation in a year. Economic growth is measured by successive rises in real GDP over time. You cannot have economic development without economic growth. Economic development is a reference to living standards and quality of life within a nation. It is measured by successive rises in HDI over time.

If the information in the box is true which of the following is also true?

A If the GDP of a nation has increased then HDI will have also increased

B If a nation wants to improve living standards, then it should focus on economic growth

C If a nation makes more goods and services then living standards will improve

D If the HDI in a nation has increased then GDP must also have increased

Use the following information to complete Questions 19 and 20.

There are 6,000,000 people on a database. The database is hacked, the data breach affected 20,000 people. Of these 8,500 are female and the rest are male.

Davis: If you are on on the database there is a 1 in 300 chance of being affected

Marie: As a female there is a 1 in 8,500 chance I was affected

Bryan: As a male there is a 23 out of 12,000 chance I was affected

Lori: As a female who has been told my data may be in breach there may be 17 chances out of 40 that I have been affected

George: This only affects 1 in every 300 people. I live on a street of 600 people so two will have been affected by the data breach.

Question 19

Which of the following is true?

A Only Bryan and Lori are correct

B Only Marie, Davis, Lori and Bryan are correct

C Only Davis and Bryan are correct

D Only Davis, Lori and Bryan are correct

Question 20

What is the **mistake** in George's reasoning?

A George does not know which of his neighbours has been affected

B George may not know the actual number of people living on his street

C George has taken the average and applied it inaccurately

D George should have said the breach affects 1 in every 3,000 people

Question 21

Unauthorised users can breach an organisation's network through attacking a user (human) vulnerability or a system vulnerability. It can do so by using one of the following attack vectors, listed in order of most important to least important:

- Username and password breaches coming from user error
- Password theft
- An inside person working against the organisation
- Unencrypted data – meaning it is readable by people it should be hidden from
- System design error

Xavier's computer is hacked.

Which of the following is the **most likely** reason?

A Xavier works beside someone who cannot be trusted

B Xavier made an error

C Xavier's organisation has a poorly designed network

D Xavier used the incorrect password

Question 22

Which of the following cannot be made into a 3D shape, **without any sides overlapping**?

A

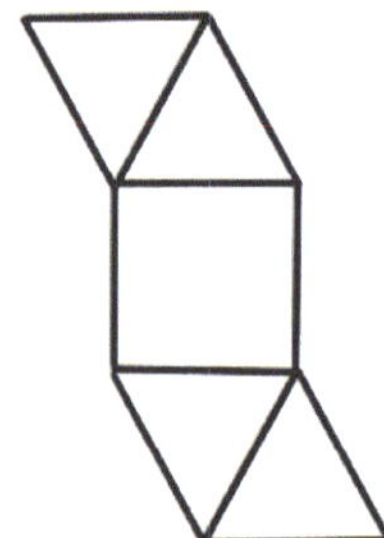

B

C

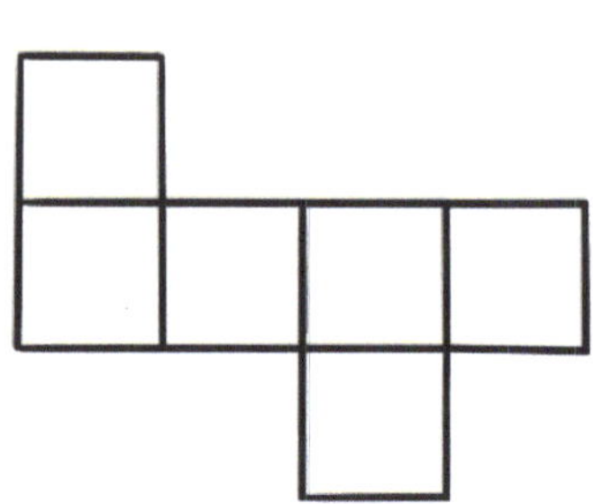

D

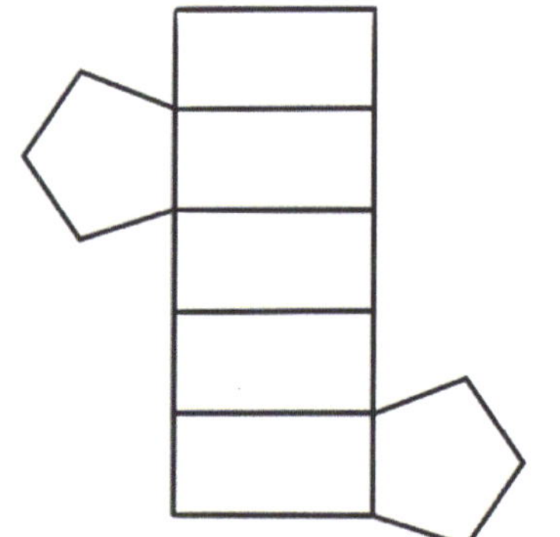

Question 23

Anais and Arun want to equally share a cupcake. Rochelle cuts it into two pieces. Arun takes a piece and Anais takes the other piece. Arun's piece is larger than Anais' piece.

Anais: That's not fair. Arun got the bigger half.

Rochelle: That does not make sense.

Which of the following is correct?

A Neither of them is right

B Both of them are right

C Only Rochelle is right

D Only Anais is right

Use the following information to complete Questions 24 and 25.

The following code is used to rate social media blogs written by bloggers:

$A^+ = 1$	$B^+ = 4$	$C^+ = 7$	$D^+ = 10$	$E^+ = 13$
A = 2	B = 5	C = 8	D = 11	E = 14
$A^- = 3$	$B^- = 6$	$C^- = 9$	$D^- = 12$	$E^- = 15$

The most popular social media blogger, with the **lowest score**, will win the prize.

Blogger	Week 1	Week 2	Week 3	Week 4	Week 5
Alicia	A^+	C^+	D^+	C^+	A^-
Ha	B^-	A^+	C^+	A^+	D^-
Paola	A^-	D	B	B^+	C^+
Loan	B^+	A^+	E^-	C	A^+
Krupa	C	A	C^-	C^+	A

Question 24

After Week 4 which of the bloggers is coming third?

A Alicia

B Ha

C Paola

D Krupa

Question 25

If Ha scored a C^+ in Week 6, what will each other blogger need to tie with Ha?

A Alicia B^- Paola B^+ Loan B^+ Krupa B^-

B Alicia B Paola B^+ Loan B^+ Krupa B^-

C Alicia B^- Paola C^+ Loan B Krupa B^-

D Alicia B^- Paola B^+ Loan B Krupa B^-

Question 26

The standard of proof in a criminal case is beyond reasonable doubt. This means a case is proven if there is no doubt. In this circumstance the accused is to be found guilty. This will be decided by the evidence and the facts established in the trial.

If there is doubt, the standard of proof has not been reached and the verdict must be not guilty. This does not mean that the accused is innocent. The accused might have committed the crime – but the court could not prove it, based on the evidence brought.

Falsi was accused of a crime and was been found not guilty by a court.

Which of the following is true?

A Falsi was proven innocent by the court

B The court found Falsi not guilty beyond reasonable doubt

C There was not enough evidence to prove Falsi was guilty

D There was some doubt raised in the evidence against Falsi

Question 27

It is not only spiders that spin webs. Many insects also make silk:

- Ants and beetles
- Wasps and bees
- Moths and caterpillars

However, unlike spiders, these insects create their silk from salivary glands. All insect and spider silks are made from protein. Spiders can create different types of silk and uses them for different purposes. Insects can only produce one type of silk each.

If the information provided above is factual, which of the following is correct?

A If silk is found to have been made by saliva, it will have been made by an insect.

B If silk was analysed and found to be made of protein it was made by a spider.

C If silk is in a web it will have been made by a spider.

D If a creature makes different types of silk, it must be a spider or insect.

Question 28

Douglas lives on a farm called "Doug's Farm". The path from the main road to his house is an unsealed dirt road Douglas can take any one of these four roads into the town.

- Coleman Highway is sealed and goes through Jessie's Farm
- Guringi Road is unsealed and goes through the pine forest
- Sullivan Road is sealed and goes past Minnie's Orchard
- Mulli Gully Way is unsealed and goes through Tania's Bluberry Farm

Unsealed roads get muddy when it rains. Douglas washed his car and heads into town. When he arrives, his car is muddy.

Which of the following does **not** logically explain this?

A It rained on Doug's Farm before he drove to town

B It rained in the pine forest as Douglas drove to town

C Doug drove through Jessie's Farm on his way to town

D Doug drove via Tania's Bluberry Farm on his way to town

Question 29

There are 3,500 personnel in the armed forces. 2,500 are soldiers. 1,830 personnel can fly planes. 760 personnel are not soldiers, and also cannot fly planes.

How many of the personnel can only fly planes?

A 2,740

B 1,590

C 910

D 240

Question 30

A "double coincidence of wants" is the basis of barter. When two parties have what the other wants then they can make an effective exchange. This will occur if the relative value of each thing being exchanged can be established and agreed.

Don: This means if I have what you want and you have what I want then we can exchange with one another.

John: My brother gave me the soccer ball he didn't want. A few weeks later it was needed for a game of soccer I had at a friend's barbeque. It was great he gave it to me. I love barter.

Who demonstrates correct reasoning?

A Don only

B John only

C Both Don and John

D Neither Don nor John

Question 31

This serial code follows a pattern.

AG2416PDB

Belle is writing on a piece of paper when her pen leaks ink over the next serial number.

What is the complete code?

A BH3636JFC

B BH3936JIC

C BH3525YEC

D BH3279QEB

Question 32

Jana's house is on Loxum Road. Jana leaves her house, turns left and runs to the end of the road and back. On her run Jana either crosses or passes 16 intersections. She does not cross Loxum Road.

On the way to the end of Loxum Road

- Davis Close is to her left. When Jana crosses this she has already passed two other streets. Immediately after Davis Close, Jana passes Len Lane to her right.
- Wurri Wurri Road is on the same side as Roseley Road.
- Jana crosses Elyard Place after passing Len Lane.
- Jammu Parade is the last intersection Jana encounters before turning back at the end of Loxum Road.

On the way back home

- The first road Jana passes on her left is Wurri Wurri Road.
- Prem Street is the closest intersection to Jana's house, just after Mittal Avenue
- Three intersections are on her side of Loxum Road and the rest are on the other side of Loxum Road

Which is the 11th intersection that Jana encounters on her run?

A Mittal Avenue

B Len Lane

C Roseley Road

D Prem Street

Question 33

Look closely at the tiles below.

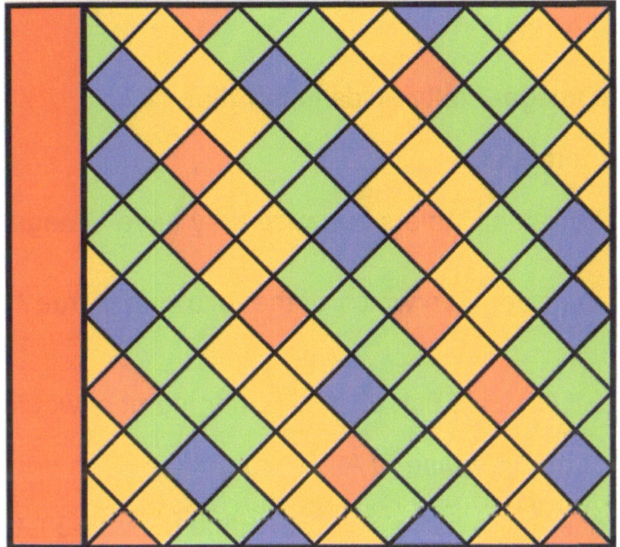

Which of the following completes the tile pattern that is covered by the red block?

A

B

C

D

Question 34

It is known that fish oil contains Omega-3 fatty acids. Omega-3 fatty acids are in the human brain. A scientific study linked low Omega-3 fatty acid levels in a diet with possible memory loss.

Alisa has low levels of Omega-3 fatty acids in her diet.

Alisa: I am sometimes forgetful.

Bonnie: You should take fish oil tablets because they have Omega-3 fatty acids.

If the first bolded lines are true, then which of the following is true?

A Bonnie is correct as if Alisa ate fish oil tablets her memory would improve

B Bonnie is not correct as the cause of Alisa's forgetfulness is not known

C Bonnie is not correct as Alisa has a diet with some Omega-3 fatty acids

D Bonnie is correct as Alisa's memory loss is probably due to low Omega-3 levels

Question 35

If Roberta works overtime she gets extra pay. If Roberta leaves early her pay is reduced. If Roberta works on weekend days her pay is increased. If Roberta is absent without notice her pay is lower. If Roberta works as a supervisor she gets increased pay.

This week, Roberta received extra pay.

Which of the following **does not** explain the reason?

A Roberta worked all Saturday and Sunday

B Roberta worked additional hours

C Roberta was asked to stay for overtime

D Roberta replaced the supervisor

Question 36

Look carefully at the pieces below.

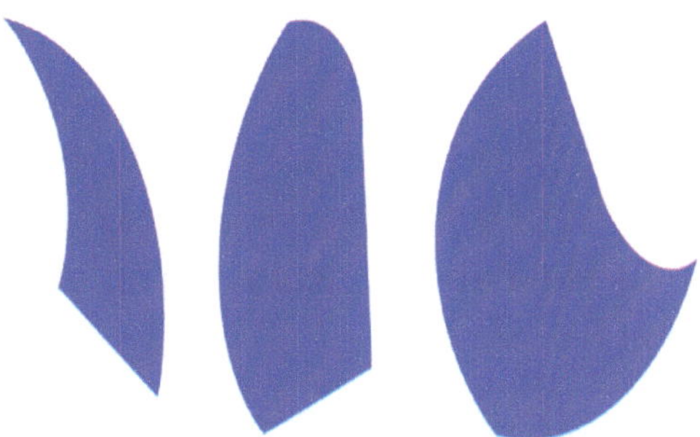

They fit into this ellipse.

Which of the following is the missing piece?

A

B

C

D

Question 37

Jane knows that on the ground, when she jumps up as high as she can, it takes her 0.5 seconds to land. Jane steps into a lift and presses the button to travel to another floor.

Which of the following **cannot** occur?

A If Jane jumps up as high as she can the instant the lift moves up, she will be in the air for less than 0.5 seconds

B If Jane jumps up as high as she when the lift is moving downwards at constant speed, she will be in the air for more than 0.5 seconds

C If Jane jumps up as high as she can the instant the lift moves down, she will be in the air for more than 0.5 seconds

D If Jane jumps up as high as she can the moment the lift is slowing down as it approaches an upper floor, she will be in the air for longer than 0.5 seconds

Question 38

If the stock market closes down in New York on a Friday, then the following Monday in Sydney the stock market will open lower.

If the stock market closes up in New York on Monday, then the stock market will open higher in Sydney on Wednesday.

What will happen in Sydney on Thursday if the stock market in New York on Wednesday does not close higher or lower?

A It could either go up or down

B It will neither go up nor down

C It will follow New York's Tuesday stock market trend

D It will follow New York's Wednesday morning stock market trend

Question 39

310 people were to identify their favourite form of drink. The results are shown in the table below.

Bottled Water	51	Chai Tea	53
Flat White Coffee	160	Green Tea	46

Only these four drinks were chosen. The information was entered into a spreadsheet in order to construct a pie chart. However, some of the data was incorrectly entered. Consequently, this was the pie chart that appeared on the screen.

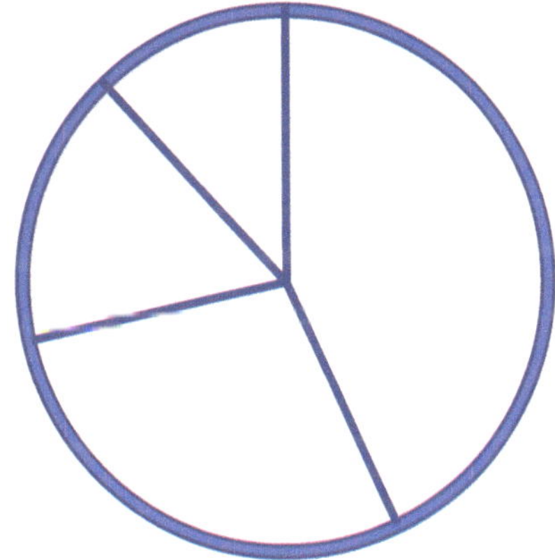

Which of the following explains the results?

A The data for Bottled Water was recorded as 105

B The data for Green Tea was recorded as 64

C The data for Flat White Coffee was recorded as 116

D The data for Chai Tea was recorded as 35

Question 40

Mohsin, standing on the 2nd floor, presses the lift button down, in order to catch the lift to the Ground Floor. The doors open and Mohsin steps inside, pressing the G button which turns orange. He is the only person in the lift.

The lift immediately heads upwards stopping at the 4th Floor where one person gets in and presses the button for the 8th Floor. The lift continues up to the 7th Floor and another person enters the lift. It then continues to the 8th Floor and these people get out leaving Mohsin alone in the lift again. He presses the already orange G button.

The lift then continues up to the 12th Floor and a person gets in, pressing the button for the 4th Floor. The lift continues down to the 5th Floor where a person gets on and presses the button to the 2nd Floor. The lift goes down to the 4th Floor where one person gets out and another person gets in. The lift goes down to the 2nd Floor and one person gets out and another gets in. This person entering the lift presses the button for the 3rd Floor.

The lift goes down to Ground Floor where Mohsin gets out.

Based on what **he experienced**, which hypothesis by Mohsin is sound?

A The lift will always prioritise a person on a higher floor going down than a person on a lower floor going up.

B The person catching the lift up from the 4th Floor pressed the lift button before Mohsin did.

C The lift will always go up before it goes down.

D The lift moves to the top of the building and then to the bottom of the building and then back to the top of the building, and so on, regardless of which floor a person wants to go to.

Question 41

Look closely at the pattern below:

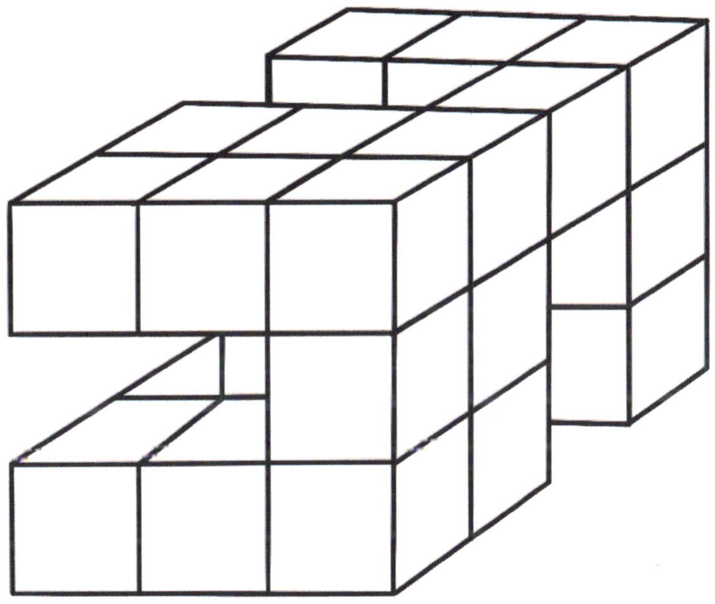

How many cubes ***cannot*** be in this shape?

A 20

B 29

C 19

D 24

Question 42

A placebo is a fake medicine that has no health effect. It is given to people who are sick in order to test the effect of patient thinking on recovery. The patient must be told, and believe, that they are taking a real medicine.

To test the effectiveness of a new medicine there are three different groups of people used in an experiment.

- **Group 1** uses the new medicine
- **Group 2** uses a placebo
- **Group 3** does not use any medicine at all.

The results are shown below.

	Number of Persons	Number who fully recovered in 3 days	Number who fully recovered in 7 days
Group 1	200	50	100
Group 2	200	40	80
Group 3	200	30	50

Which of the following can be concluded from the experiment results?

A It is better to use fake medicine than no medicine.

B The new medicine will make all people recover within 14 days.

C People using a placebo recover faster than those using nothing.

D If people think they will get better then they will heal faster.

Question 43

Look closely at the tile pattern presented below.

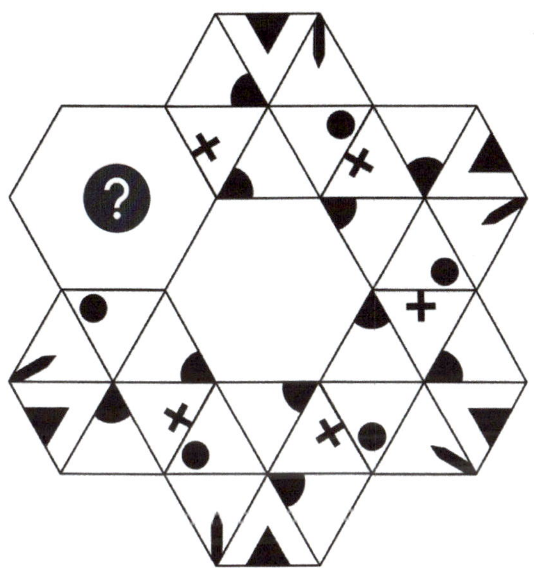

Which panel should replace the 

A

B

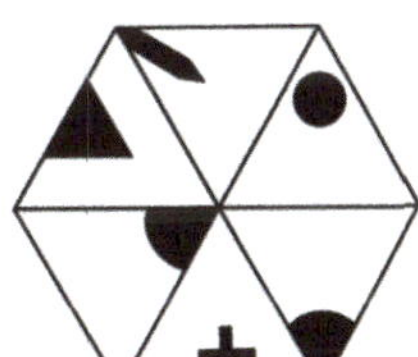

C

D

Question 44

In order to analyse you need to be able to explain. In order to describe you need to be able to recall. In order to evaluate you need to be able to show the link between cause and effect. Evaluate means to make a judgment based on criteria. Explain means to show the link between cause and effect. Describe means to provide the characteristics and features of something. If you can show the link between cause and effect, then you can also provide the characteristics and features of something.

Dani is able to analyse things well, which of the following is NOT necessarily true?

A Dani can provide the characteristics and features of things

B Dani is able to recall

C Dani can show the link between cause and effect

D Dani can make a judgment based on criteria

Question 45

Look closely at the pattern in the stained-glass window shown below.

Which of the following arrangements completes the pattern on the stained-glass?

A

B

C

D

Question 46

This tile pattern was on the wall of an art gallery.

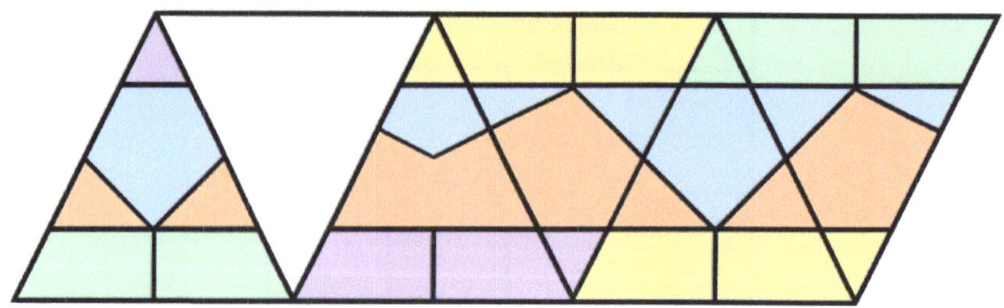

One of the tiles was removed.

Which of the following is the removed tile?

A

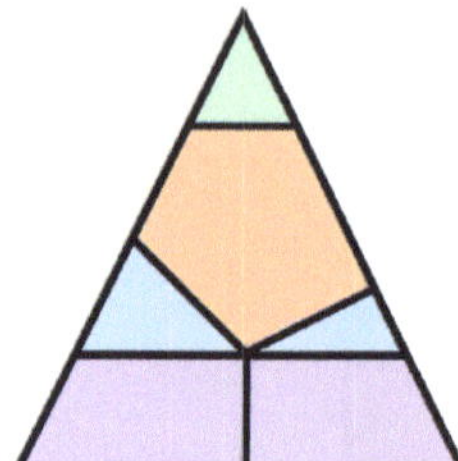

B

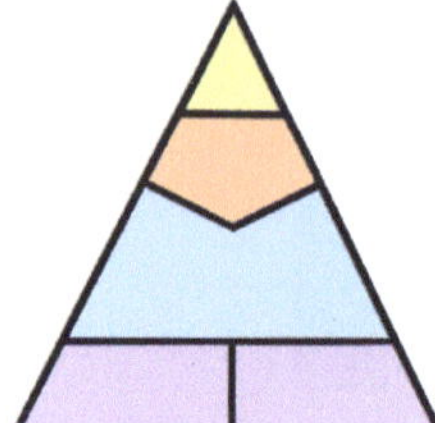

C

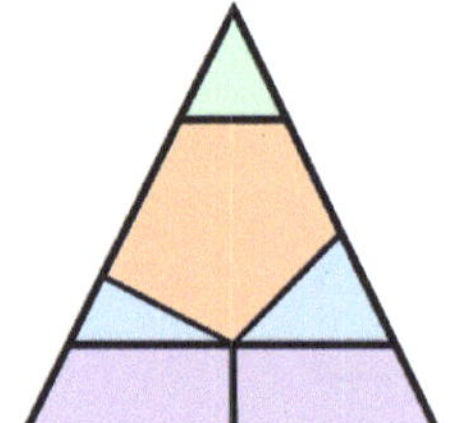

D

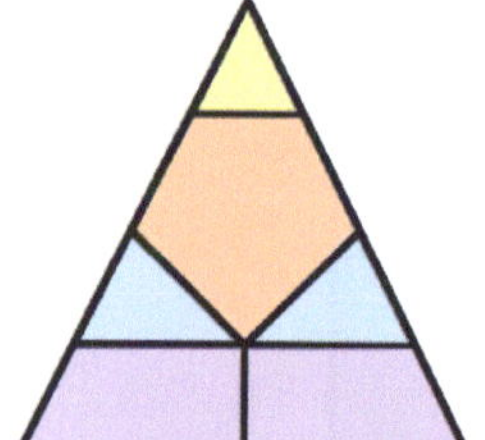

Question 47

When this shape is viewed from the top what would be seen?

Top view

Bottom view

A

B

C

D

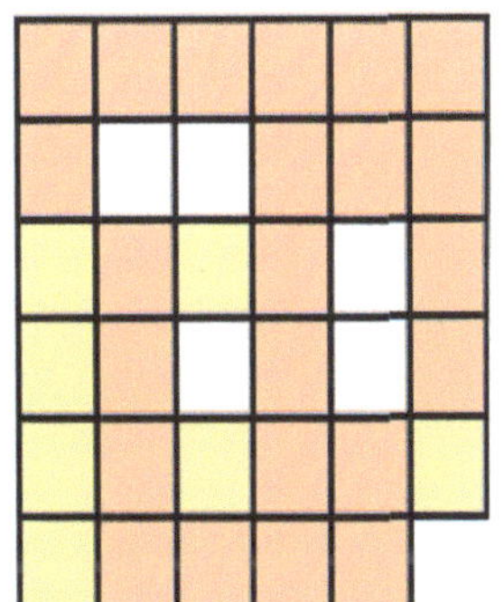

Question 48

Facts

1. Mammals are warm blooded. They maintain their own internal body temperature.
2. Mammals give birth to live young. The young are not born out of eggs. They develop in the uterus of the body of a parent.
3. Mammals have fur or hair.
4. Mammals suckle their young – meaning their young take milk from mammary glands
5. Mammals breathe air through lungs.
6. Mammals have a single piece lower jaw.
7. Mammals mostly have one time tooth replacement. That is, they are mostly diphyodonts.
8. Mammals have three bones in the inner ear: the hammer, the anvil and the stirrup.
9. Mammals have four-chambered hearts.

Additional facts

1. Birds have four-chambered hearts.
2. Kangaroos do not have one time tooth replacement.
3. Whales have hair.
4. Birds lay eggs.

Based on the information provided above, which of the following is correct?

A It can be hypothesised that as birds have four-chambered hearts they are mammals

B It can be hypothesised that as kangaroos are not diphyodonts they cannot be mammals

C It can be hypothesised that as salamanders breathe air, they are mammals

D It can be hypothesised that as whales have hair, they are mammals

Question 49

A wall is painted with the following pattern for a festival.

Which of these is the correct arrangement of colours for the part that needs to be painted?

A

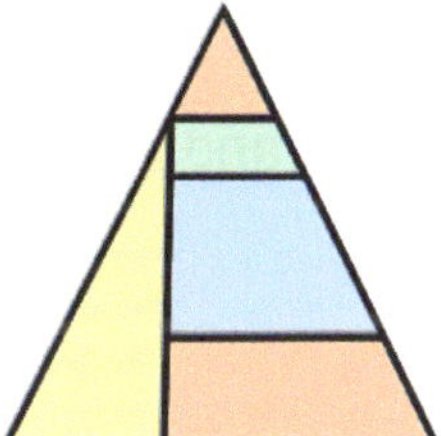

B

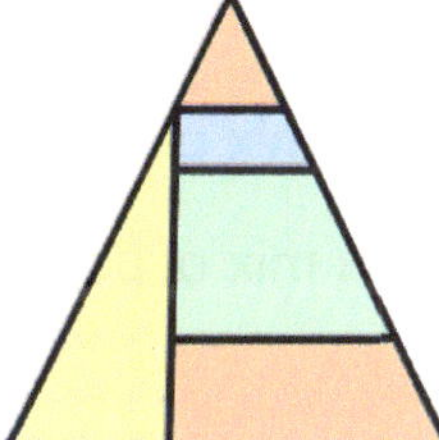

C

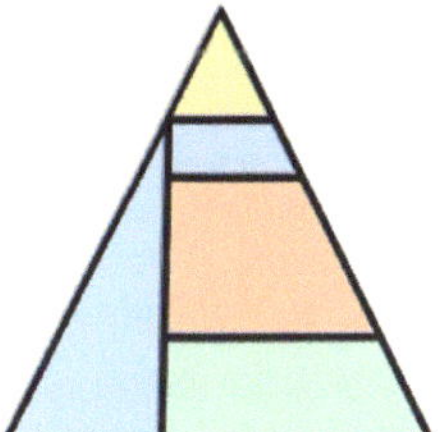

D

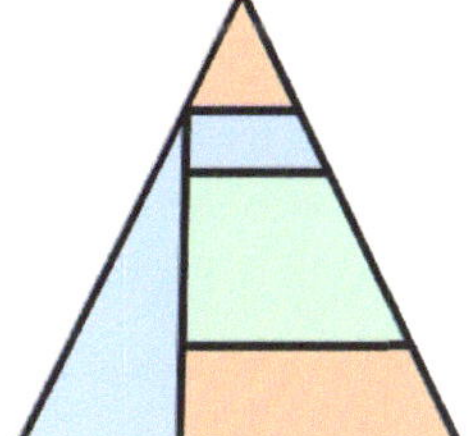

Question 50

There are three different kinds of tears: basal tears, reflex tears and emotional tears. Basal tears keep the eyes clean and protect them. They contain water, oil, mucus and electrolytes. Basal tears are always coating eyes so that they remain clean. Reflex tears are also called irritant tears and occur in response to protect the eyes from foreign particles or vapours – such as smoke or chemicals. Emotional tears are associated with human feelings. Emotional tears contain more proteins and hormones than the other kinds of tears.

Kepler is cutting onions when he hears a story about a man who lost his dog. This story deeply upsets Kepler. Kepler is observed to have tears.

Which of the following can be concluded about Kepler's tears?

A Kepler's tears will be in response to the onion vapours or might contain more hormones than usual.

B Kepler's tears will be emotional tears as Kepler is deeply upset about the man losing his dog.

C Kepler's tears will be a mix of all three kinds of tears: basal, reflex and emotional.

D Kepler's tears will be a mix of basal tears and irritant tears.

Question 51

In a vehicle sales yard there are motorbikes, cars and trucks. There are 37 vehicles in the yard. The motorbikes have 2 wheels, the cars have 4 wheels, and the trucks have 6 wheels. Kalia counts the total number of wheels in the sales yard, and it totals 136.

If there are four trucks in the yard, how many motorbikes are there?

A 10

B 23

C 33

D 46

Question 52

There are 255 children at a park. 148 of the children wear a short-sleeved shirt. 170 of the children wear hats. 43 people do not wear hats or wear a short-sleeved shirt.

How many children wear hats but do not have a short-sleeved shirt on?

A 212

B 42

C 106

D 64

Question 53

There are 80 sheep on a farm.

65 sheep get shorn between 1 January and April 30. 45 sheep get shorn between the start of April and June.

How many sheep are shorn in April?

A 15

B 30

C 35

D 45

Use the following information to do Question 54 and 55.

Nolan gets his salary paid on Thursday every fortnight. This year he gets paid three salary payments in two different months. This happens first in April. Nolan's first April pay is made on the first day of the month.

Question 54

Which is the next month when Nolan will receive three fortnightly payments?

A October

B September

C August

D Juy

Question 55

2024 is a leap year with January commencing on a Monday. He's paid in the first week of January. In which months would Nolan get 3 pays?

A January and February

B February and July

C February and August

D February and May

Question 56

When the virus pandemic started, the queues for the supermarket were longer than anyone in Sydney had ever seen. There was panic buying ahead of a lockdown, with people being told they would have to remain at home for a week.

When a supermarket chain called BuyIt has special discounts there are long queues outside its Sydney stores.

Yesterday evening there was a government announcement that a new virus had been detected in Sydney.

Anya: I saw the longest queues I have ever seen outside BuyIt this morning. People must be panic buying.

Monya: Maybe there was a new special discount.

Anya: Today? After a virus announcement? I don't think so.

Based on the information, who is correct?

A Anya only

B Monya only

C Both Anya and Monya

D Neither Anya nor Monya

Question 57

Djarko runs on the path shown below, starting at point A. His path takes him beside a golf course. Djarko passes three houses which have dogs. When he is at point B, Dog 2 barks twice. When he is at point D, Dog 3 barks twice. When he runs back, the dogs bark at exactly the same points on his path. No other dogs bark.

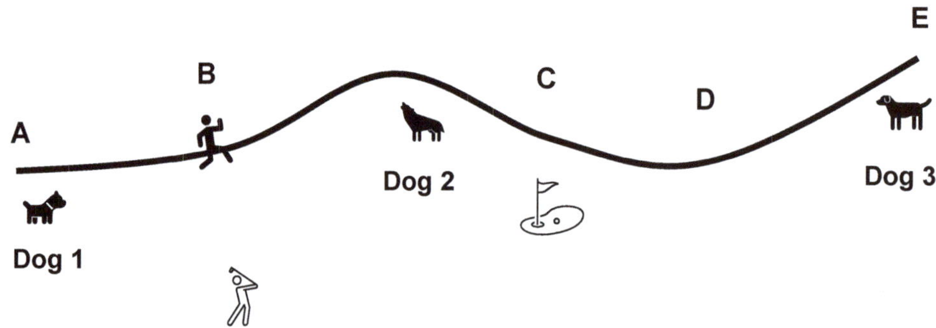

Which hypothesis made by Djarko is sustained **by this evidence?**

A Dogs respond to his smell and bark

B Dogs always bark twice when they first see him

C Dogs bark at him and the golfer

D Dogs always bark twice when they hear him

Question 58

There are no reptiles that are not cold blooded.
There are no reptiles that do not breathe oxygen.
There are no vertebrate fish that are not cold blooded.
There are no vertebrate fish that do not breathe oxygen.

If these statements are true, then which statement is untrue?

A As chameleons are reptiles, they must be cold blooded

B If it is cold blooded it could be a vertebrate fish

C If it breathes oxygen, it could be a reptile or a vertebrate fish

D In a group of oxygen breathing animals there will be reptiles and vertebrate fish

Question 59

While running in a children's park, Mohsin noticed that a child standing beside an adult did not move even though he was running straight towards the child. Mohsin, ran off the path and back onto it to run around them. Later on, he noticed that as he ran towards a man and a child, who was holding the man's hand, the child did not move. He again ran off the path to go around the pair. As he finished, he saw a child run to get a ball by crossing the path, immediately in front of another person who was running.

Which of the following is **an incorrect hypothesis** based on these events?

A Children cannot perceive the speed of oncoming runners

B Children with their parents feel safe

C Children in parks do not perceive oncoming safety threats

D Children are in parks focus on what they are doing

Question 60

Look closely at the pattern below.

Which panel should replace this: 

A

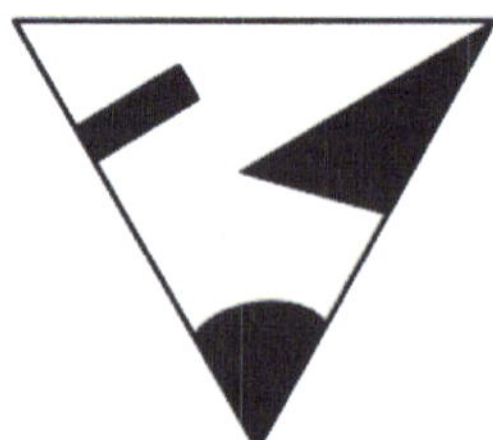

B

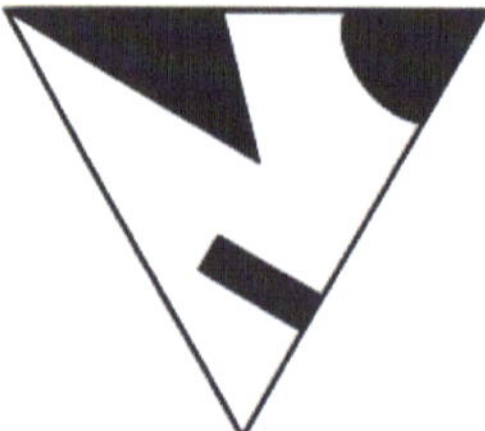

C

D

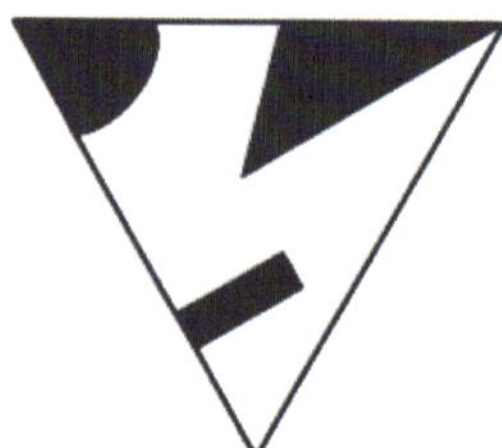

Answers

Answers

Summary of Answers

1	A	11	D	21	B	31	A	41	C	51	A
2	B	12	B	22	B	32	C	42	C	52	D
3	D	13	A	23	C	33	B	43	B	53	B
4	C	14	C	24	A	34	B	44	D	54	B
5	C	15	A	25	D	35	C	45	C	55	C
6	C	16	C	26	D	36	D	46	C	56	B
7	A	17	B	27	A	37	B	47	A	57	A
8	B	18	D	28	C	38	C	48	D	58	D
9	A	19	C	29	D	39	A	49	B	59	B
10	D	20	C	30	D	40	A	50	A	60	A

A = 1, 7, 9, 13, 15, 24, 27, 31, 39, 40, 47, 50, 51, 57, 60

B = 2, 8, 12, 17, 21, 22, 33, 34, 37, 43, 49, 53, 54, 56, 59

C = 4, 5, 6, 14, 16, 19, 20, 23, 28, 32, 35, 38, 41, 42, 45, 55

D = 3, 10, 11, 18, 25, 26, 29, 30, 36, 44, 48, 52, 58

Fully worked solutions

Question 1

A

Applying the given rules, the aircraft will land in the following order:

<table>
<tr><td>1</td><td>Helicopter 2 – an emergency vehicle</td><td rowspan="2">It can be argued that this order could be reversed given that Aircraft 3 is already preparing to land.</td></tr>
<tr><td>2</td><td>Aircraft 3 – An international flight</td></tr>
<tr><td>3</td><td colspan="2">Aircraft 5 – Another international flight</td></tr>
<tr><td>4</td><td colspan="2">Aircraft 4 or Aircraft 7 – One of the domestic flights. However, Aircraft 4 will land first as it is closer to South-East</td></tr>
<tr><td>5</td><td colspan="2">Aircraft 7 – the other domestic flight.</td></tr>
<tr><td>6</td><td colspan="2">Aircraft 1 – a helicopter that is not an emergency vehicle.</td></tr>
<tr><td>7</td><td colspan="2">Aircraft 6 – A light aircraft, which will land after Aircraft 6 – a helicopter that is not an emergency vehicle.</td></tr>
</table>

Question 2

B

The main argument here is that Mark is independent and likes to learn through experimentation. Consequently, A is irrelevant. C is a statement about "many young people" but is not specific to characteristics that may apply to Mark. D relies on inductive reasoning, but here the implication drawn is incorrect. Firstly, we do not know what the sign was referring to. Secondly, that Mark climbed the tree does not mean he was experimenting. B is correct as Mark's attempt indicates he was unsure of the outcome – as is the case with experimentation.

Question 3

D

Brenda's argument is that wood can be harder than steel. This does not necessarily mean that wood can replace steel, nor that it is stronger when used in different contexts. Hence A does not add to the argument.

B is opinion, albeit probably informed. It is however not expert opinion. C does not add to the argument. Indeed, if true it weakens Brenda's argument.

D is correct as if steel nails cannot be hammered into hardwood trees the wood is harder than the steel, and this is consistent with, and strengths Brenda's argument.

Question 4

C

	Starting position	**First toss** Heads Tom $2-coin	**Second toss** Tail Sandy $1-coin	**Third toss** Heads Daniel 50-cent coin
		Player has to give each of the others 5 lollies	Player receives 3 lollies from each of the other players	Player has to give each of the others 3 lollies
Tom	40	25	22 (-3)	**25 (+3)**
Sandy	40	45 (+5)	54 (+9)	**57 (+3)**
Daniel	40	45 (+5)	42 (-3)	**33 (-9)**
Kuong	40	45 (+5)	42 (-3)	**45 (+3)**

Hence C is correct.

Question 5

C

After one full set of coin tosses the players have this number of lollies:

Tom: 44 lollies **Sandy 44 lollies** **Daniel 20 lollies** **Kuong 52 lollies**

	Start	**First toss** Tom $2-coin Tail	**Second toss** Tail Sandy $1-coin	**Third toss** Heads Daniel 50-cent coin	**Fourth toss** Tails Kuong 20-cent coin
		Player receives 3 lollies from each of the other players	Player receives 3 lollies from each of the other players	Player has to give each of the others 3 lollies	Player receives 5 lollies from each of the other players
Tom	40	49 (+9)	46 (-3)	49 (+3)	**44 (-5)**
Sandy	40	37 (-3)	46 (+9)	49 (+3)	**44 (-5)**
Daniel	40	37 (-3)	34 (-3)	25 (-9)	**20 (-5)**
Kuong	40	37 (-3)	34 (-3)	37 (+3)	**52 (+15)**

For completeness – calculate all of the other options

A. Tom: Tail, Sandy: Head, Daniel: Head, Kuong: Tail

After each of the coins is tossed, this arrangement gives:

Tom: 51 lollies, Sandy 23 lollies, Daniel: 27 lollies and Kuong 49 lollies

	$2-coin **Tom-Tail**	$1-coin **Sandy-Head**	50-cent coin **Daniel-Head**	20-cent coin **Kuong-Tail**
T	49 (+9)	53 (+4)	56 (+3)	**51 (-5)**
S	37 (-3)	25 (-12)	28 (+3)	**23 (-5)**
D	37 (-3)	41 (+4)	32 (-9)	**27 (-5)**
K	37 (-3)	41 (+4)	44 (+3)	**59 (+15)**

B. Tom: Head, Sandy: Head, Daniel: Head, Kuong: Head

After each of the coins is tossed, this arrangement gives:

	$2-coin **Tom-Head**	$1-coin **Sandy-Head**	50-cent coin **Daniel-Head**	20-cent coin **Kuong-Head**
T	25 (-15)	29 (+4)	32 (+3)	**35 (+3)**
S	45 (+5)	33 (-12)	36 (+3)	**39 (+3)**
D	45 (+5)	49 (+4)	40 (-9)	**43 (+3)**
K	45 (+5)	49 (+4)	52 (+3)	**43 (-9)**

Tom: 35 lollies, Sandy 39 lollies, Daniel: 43 lollies and Kuong 43 lollies

D. Tom: Tail, Sandy: Tail, Daniel: Head, Kuong: Head

After each of the coins is tossed, this arrangement gives:

	$2-coin **Tom-Tail**	$1-coin **Sandy-Tail**	50-cent coin **Daniel-Head**	20-cent coin **Kuong-Head**
T	49 (+9)	46 (-3)	49 (+3)	**52 (+3)**
S	37 (-3)	46 (+9)	49 (+3)	**52 (+3)**
D	37 (-3)	34 (-3)	25 (-9)	**28 (+3)**
K	37 (-3)	34 (-3)	37 (+3)	**28 (-9)**

Therefore these tosses give this arrangement:
Tom: 52 lollies, Sandy 52 lollies, Daniel: 28 lollies and Kuong 28 lollies

Question 6

C

After each person has tossed their coins, it goes back to Tom and they all toss again and **again in the same order**.

If the coin tosses are: H, T, H, T, H, T, H, H, T, T, H, T, T, T then which person is the first to have no lollies left?

Daniel – as can be seen from the table below.

Coin	$2	$1	50c	20c	$2	$1	50c	20c	$2	$1	50c	20c	$2	$1
Side	H	T	H	T	H	T	H	H	T	T	H	T	T	T
Tosser	T	S	D	K	T	S	D	K	T	S	D	K	T	S
Tom	25	22	25	20	5	2	5	8	17	14	17	12	21	18
Sandy	45	54	57	52	57	66	69	72	69	78	81	76	73	**80***
Daniel	45	42	33	28	33	30	21	24	21	18	9	4	1	-
Kuong	45	42	45	60	65	62	65	56	53	50	53	68	65	62

* Sandy can only receive 7 lollies as Daniel can only give 1 lolly, not 3.

Question 7

A

The players decide to alter the rules so that the amounts they give or receive is doubled. **They toss again in the same order, Tom, Sandy, Daniel and Kuong.**

Who has 24 lollies after this pattern of coin throws? T, T, H, T, H, H, T, H

Tom has 24 lollies as can be seen below.

Coin	$2	$1	50c	20c	$2	$1	50c	20c
Side	T	T	H	T	H	H	T	H
Tosser	T	S	D	K	T	S	D	K
Tom	58	52	58	48	18	26	18	24
Sandy	34	52	58	48	58	34	26	32
Daniel	34	28	10	-	10	18	42	48
Kuong	34	28	34	64	74	82	74	56

Question 8

B

Since:

Blue and Yellow = Green, so A = Yellow as is G, and C must be Blue.

Orange and Indigo = Green, so B = Indigo.

E must be Green.

Red and Violet = Green, hence F = Violet.

So what about D?

We have from Left to Right the following unaccounted for pegs:

The first Red one, peg D and the final TWO pegs on the right hand side: Orange and Indigo (which together add to Green).

Hence the Red peg must be matched to Violet – hence D is Violet.

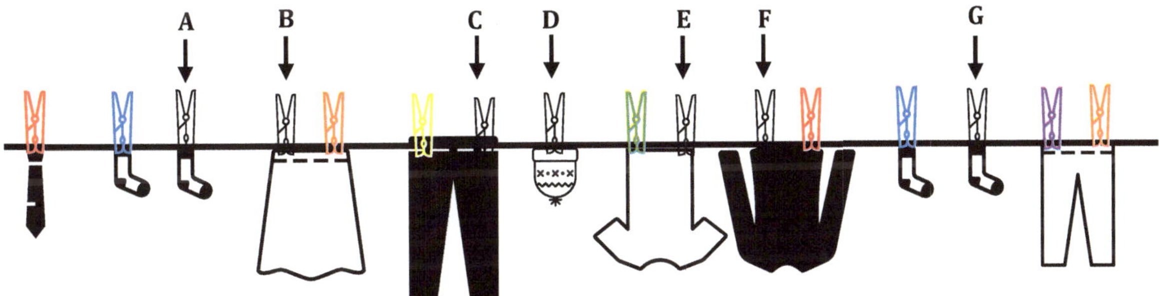

The order therefore is as shown in B:

A: Yellow, B: Indigo, C: Blue, D: Violet, E: Green, F: Violet and G: Yellow

Question 9

A

First understand the values for the symbols

= 1 (red peg)

= 2 (orange peg)

= 3 (yellow peg)

= 4 (green peg)

= 5 (blue peg)

= 6 (indigo peg)

= 7 (violet peg)

This shown within the boxes below.

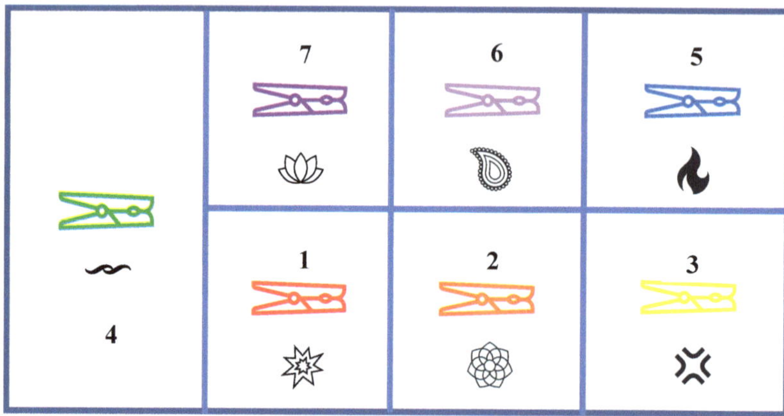

Which of these does NOT represent columns of equal value?

A 7 and 4 and [3 + 6]

7 x 4 = 28 and 4 x 7 = 28 and [3 x 2 + 6 x 6] = 42 Hence not equal

B 5 and [2 + 5] and [3 + 4]

5 x 5 = 25 and [2 x 5 + 5 x 3] = 25 and [3 x 7 + 4 x 1] = 25. All are equal

C [6 +] and 3 and [2 + 4]

[6 x 2 + 6] = 18 and 3 x 6 = 18 and [2 x 7 + 4 x 1] = 18. All are equal.

D [8 +] and [7 + 2.5] and [4 +]

[8 x 3 + 5] = 29 and [7 x 2 + 2.5 x 6] =29 and [4 x 7 + 1] = 29. All are equal.

Hence A is correct.

Answers

Question 10

D

Solution

R = 1, O = 2, Y = 3, G = 4, B = 5, I = 6, V = 7

Hence:

V,VYG,RGB,IVO,RBI
7,734,145,672,156

As shown in D.

Question 11

D

	Mon	Tues	Wed	Thurs	Fri	Sat	Sun
Week 1							
Run length	6 km	4 km	4 km	REST	4 km	REST	12 km
Time	31:26	19:09	18:53	-	18:48	-	70:00
Week 2							
Run length	6 km	4 km	REST	REST	4 km	REST	14 km
Time	32:00	19.02	-	-	18:21	-	80:00
Week 3							
Run length	6 km	4 km	REST	4 km	4 km	REST	16 km
Time	32:30	18:58	-	18:25	18:11	-	90:00
Week 4							
Run length	6 km	4 km	REST	4 km	4 km	REST	12 km
Time	33:30	18:23	-	18:07	17:55	-	59:20
Week 5							
Run length	6 km	4 km	4 km	REST	4 km	REST	14 km
Time	31:23	19:07	18:55	-	18:42	-	81:00

What **cannot** be **hypothesised** from the data presented?

Taking each of the answers in turn:

A: Running times on Mondays are slower per kilometre due to the Sunday long run. This is possible as it is evident that as the Sunday runs lengthen the Monday runs are slower.

B: As Sunday runs get longer the fastest 4 km times get lower. This is also possible as there appears to be a relationship between the increasing distance on Sundays and the fastest 4 km times.

C: 4 km runs on Tuesday are slowest because of the previous days of running: This is possible as Tuesday runs are the slowest runs in the week and come after 2 days of running.

D: A fourth 4 km run on Saturdays will be faster than the 4 km runs on Fridays. This cannot be known or even hypothesised as it could depend on the number of consecutive training days prior to Saturday.

Question 12

B

The data for week 6 is presented below.

Week 6							
Run length	6 km	4 km	4 km	REST	4 km	REST	14 km
Time	32:20	18:56	18.39	-	?	-	80:21

The problem with A is the **justification**. The time may be possible (probably high) but it cannot be because "it looks like week 3 repeated". The justification needs to be related to specific data to be logical.

The problem with C is similar. Whilst there may be a pattern, the pattern needs to be justified on the basis of actual data.

Now to D. The Friday run in Week 3 following a 14 km Sunday run was 18.11. However, this came after a Wednesday rest day. As a general pattern if Wednesday is rest day the Thursday and Friday times are lower. However, if it isn't the Friday time is lower. Hence the reason (the justification) is probably incorrect.

B predicts a higher time than A – consistent with the data in Weeks 1 and 5. Moreover, the justification is also consistent with the data. Hence B is correct.

Question 13

A

The shape rotates clockwise by 90 degrees in each successive panel: Top left quarter, top right quarter, bottom right quarter and bottom left quarter.

Question 14

C

A is incorrect as there has been no causal link found – it could be coincidental. B is also incorrect as this application of inductive thinking leads to the incorrect conclusion. It is certainly not probably – though it is possible. This also rules out D as well.

C is correct as though the blood clots may have occurred through natural causes – and hence the condition may be coincidental, it is also possible that the vaccine caused the blood clots.

Question 15

A

Look closely at net. You can see that the top face will be opposite the 3rd face as shown with red arrows.

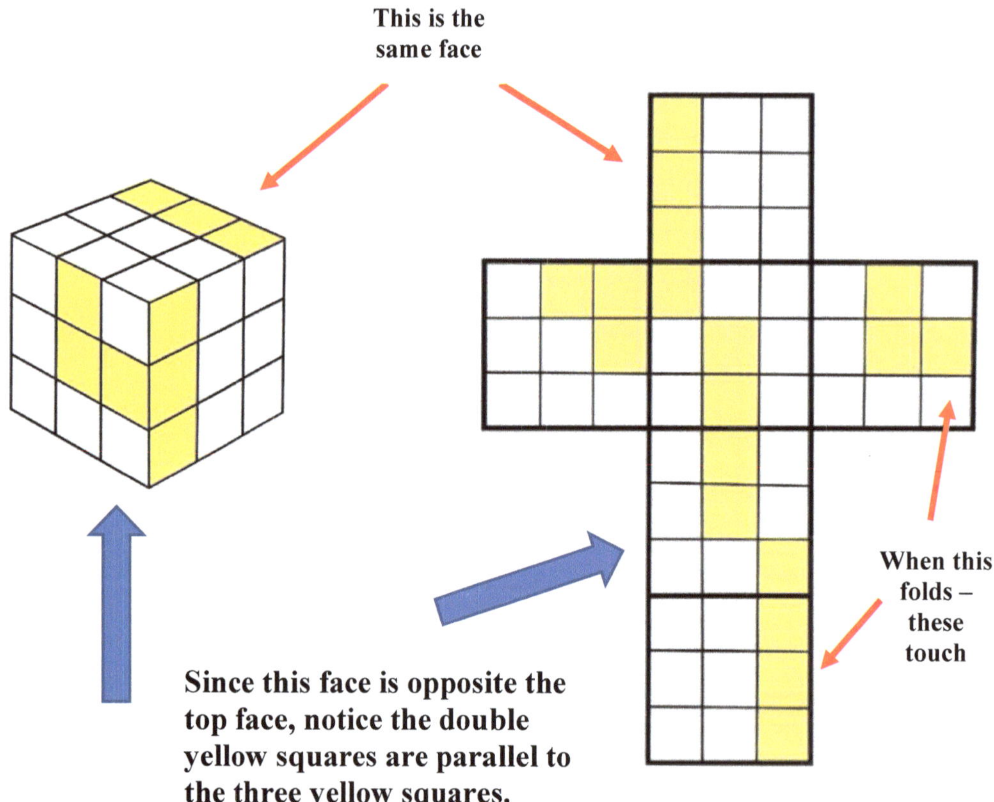

The options are:

A 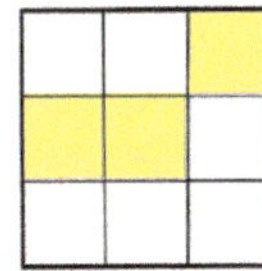

C

Rotating them gives:

A 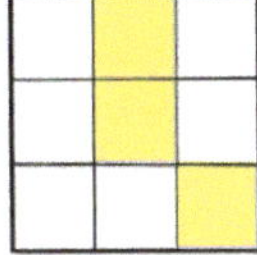

C 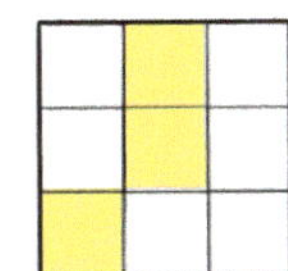

Hence A is correct.

Question 16

C

All of the options have 8 characters in length, so this does not distinguish their strengths.

With A there are repeated letters: d and D and consecutive numbers 1 and 2 and also 7 and 6. These present weaknesses.

With B we see that u and V are consecutive letters – a weakness as well.

With D there is a 4 followed by a 3 – consecutive numbers.

C has none of these weaknesses and must be the strongest of the passwords.

Question 17

B

Assessing the **weakest** passwords first: none of these is very hard to guess – at least the first words where numbers substitute letters are slightly harder (last criterion). Repeated password use is weaker than something new, notwithstanding that Jason has used names of Sally and Bertram. So, the weakest two passwords are in A and B:

jA50n23$%
jASoN123#

Of these the second is weaker than the first one as it repeats all of these characters in order: oN12. It also suffers from consecutive numbers "123".

Hence the weakest password for a change from what he had is: jASoN123#

Now to the **strongest** password.

WE can immediately rule out

C: jA50n23$% and D: jASoN123# as these are the weakest for reasons outlined earlier.

This leaves:

A: 533fJ@h2

This uses lowercase letters, numbers and special characters, but repeats the 33 and uses no uppercase letters. It is also is the shortest password with 8 characters only. All the rest have 9 characters.

B: B3rtR4M!2

This uses a mix of lower and upper case letters, numbers and a special character. It also has nine characters instead of 8.

Consequently, B has both the weakest and the strongest passwords listed.

Answers

Question 18

D

A cannot be true as the information states that you can have economic growth (or increases in GDP) without economic development (ie not change in HDI). This actually shows why B should be discounted or excluded as well. To improve living standards then changes in HDI are required nit change s in GDP. C is incorrect as to "make more goods and services" means to increase GDP. We have seen that this does not guarantee increases in living standards.

D is correct as if HDI increases, or there are rises in living standards, the economic growth must follow. The sentence says this:

You cannot have economic development without economic growth.

Question 19

C

So, let us see what the correct statistics are. If there are 6,000,000 people on a database that is hacked, affecting 20,000 people there is a one in 300 chance of any individual being affected. This is calculated as follows: 20,000 ÷ 6,000,000 or 1 in 30. Hence, Davis is correct.

Marie is not correct as there is a 85 in 60 000 or 17 in 12000 chance she was affected – not 1 in 8,500.

Bryan has a 1 in 6,000,000 chance of being personally affected. However, as a male, he knows that 11,500 males are affected from the database. Hence 11,500/6,000,000 is 115/60,000 = 23/12,000 chance of a male being affected.

Similarly, Lori applies the same logic – 8,500 females affected out of 6,000,000 people. However, her reasoning is 8,500/20,000 = 85/200 or 17/40 which is not correct. Her logic for the group of females should be is 8,500/6,000,000 = 85/60,000 = 17/12,000.

Hence only Davis and Bryan are correct as shown in C.

Question 20

C

A is not relevant. It is possible no-one on George's street has been affected. B is not relevant as the issue is one of a statistical misapplication not how many people live on his street. D is an incorrect statistic.

George is correct that 1 in 300 people are affected: 20,000 ÷ 6,000,000 = 2 ÷ 600 = 1 in 300. However, these people are highly unlikely to be equally distributed across each possible grouping of 600 people. C is correct as it details the average correctly (1 in 300) but it applies it uniformly which leads to inaccuracy.

Question 21

B

The order provided is from most important to least important. The most likely is user error. The user is Xavier hence the logical conclusions is that Xavier made an error which allowed someone to hack the computer.

Question 22

B

A (square pyramid) will have no overlapping sides. Nor will C (cube) nor D (pentagonal prism). However, B will have five overlapping sides

A

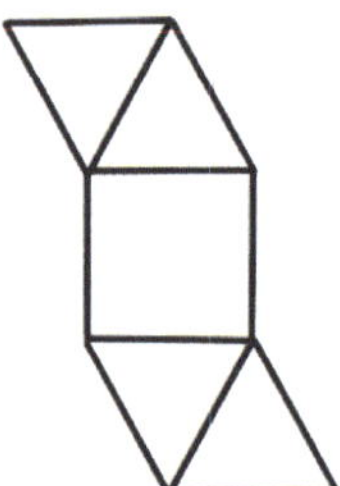

B

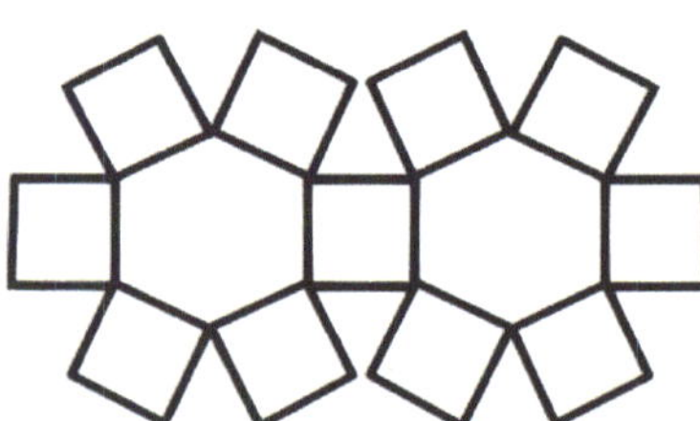

C

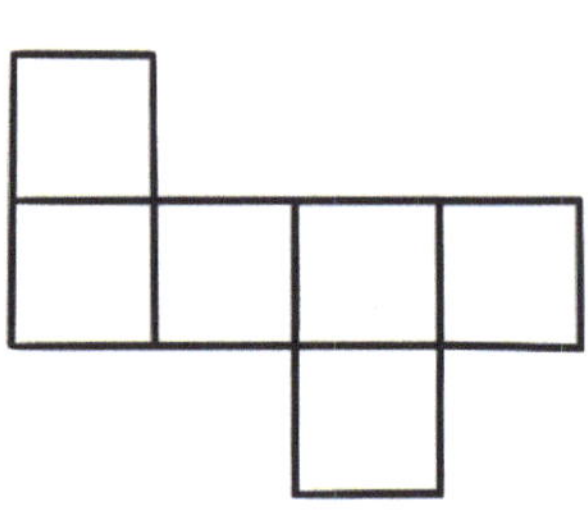

D

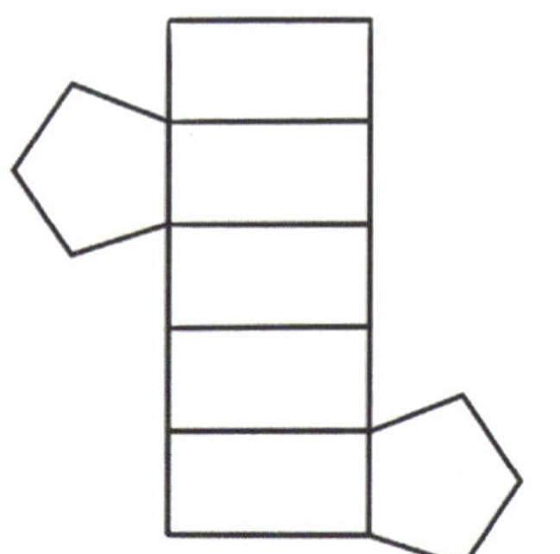

Question 23

C

Halves are equal portions. The two portions were unequal and hence cannot be halves. So, only Rochelle is correct.

Question 24

A

After Week 4 the scores are:

Alicia: 1 + 7 + 10 + 7 = 25 (third)
Ha: 6 + 1 + 7 + 1 = 15 (first)
Paola: 3 + 11 + 5 + 4 = 23 (second)
Loan: 4 + 1 + 15 + 8 = 28 (fifth)
Krupa: 8 + 2 + 9 + 7 = 26 (fourth)

Hence Alicia is coming THIRD, which is option A.

Question 25

D

After Week 5 the scores are:

Alicia: 1 + 7 + 10 + 7 + 3 = 28
Ha: 6 + 1 + 7 + 1 + 12 = 27
Paola: 3 + 11 + 5 + 4 + 7 = 30
Loan: 4 + 1 + 15 + 8 + 1 = 29
Krupa: 8 + 2 + 9 + 7 + 2 = 28

If Ha scores a C^+ in Week 6 then her score is 34.

So, this means:

Alicia will need 6 (B^-), Paola 4 (B^+), Loan 5 (B) and Krupa 6 (B^-)

This is shown in D.

Question 26

D

The court can find people either guilty or not guilty. They are not proven "innocent". Hence, A is incorrect. The standard of proof to find guilt is 'beyond reasonable doubt'. This is not a standard that applies to being not guilty. Hence B is incorrect. The evidence and the facts are required to prove guilt. In C there is a reference to evidence only. Hence C is incorrect.

D is correct because if there is any doubt the decision (verdict) given by the court must be not guilty. Hence there must have been some doubt for that finding to have been returned.

Question 27

A

Taking B first. Since ALL insect and spider silks are made of protein, then B is incorrect as it says, "it must have been made by a spider".

C is also incorrect as the introductory line says, "It is NOT only spiders that spin webs". Hence silk webs can be made by other creatures so it does not follow that a silk web "will have been made" by a spider.

D is incorrect because it says spider or insect. Insects make only one type of web, so this statement should not include insects.

From the information given, insect silk is distinguished from spider silk on the basis of how it is made: by saliva. Hence A is correct.

Question 28

C

Doug's car can only have become muddy if he drove on an unsealed road. There are three unsealed roads: the one from his house to the main road, Guringi road which goes through the pine forest and Mulli Gully Way which goes through Tania's Bluberry farm. Consequently, A, B and D do explain the mud. C however does not, as Jessie Farm is on a sealed road. Hence C is correct.

Question 29

D

Let A = the number of personnel who are ONLY soldiers.
Let B = the number of personnel who can ONLY fly planes.
Let C = the number of personnel who are soldiers AND can fly planes.

From the information provided we know that:

A + C = 2,500
B + C = 1,830
And, A + B + C = 3,500 – 760 = 2,740

Hence:

A + 1,830 = 2,740. So this means that A must be 910 personnel.
2,500 + B = 2,740 so B must be 240 personnel.
For completeness, C = 1,590 personnel.

Hence D is correct. 240 personnel can only fly planes.

Question 30

D

Neither Don nor John is correct. Don is incorrect because the barter can only occur if TWO conditions are satisfied, not one: each has what the other wants AND they can agree on value. John is incorrect as there is no evidence that he gave anything in return. There is no exchange. He received the ball but did not give anything of value in exchange.

Question 31

A

The question here is what is the pattern? A is the first letter followed by G - the 7th letter of the alphabet. The numbers that follow are 2, 2 × 2 (4) or 2^2 (4) and 4^2 (16). P is the 16th letter of the alphabet, D is the 4th and B the 2nd.

The part of the pattern that is visible is: BH3

Following the rules: BH3 is given, then 3 × 2 = 6, and then 6^2 = 36. The next letter corresponding to 36 counting from A goes 26 places to Z and then starting from A again moves another 10 places to J. The code so far is BH3636J and the last two letters in order are F matching the 6 and C, matching the 3.

Hence the pattern must be: **BH3636JFC**

This is shown in A

Question 32

C

Strategy

Read the whole scenario through. There are 16 intersections she either crosses or passes on the way out ***and back*** – hence there are 8 individual intersections.

It will also be clear from reading the whole scenario, that on Jana's side of Loxum Road there are three intersections: Davis Street, Elyard Place and Jammu Parade. There are five on the other side of Loxum Road: Len Lane, Wurri Wurri Road, Roseley Road, Prem Street and Mittal.

So, now the order

On her side of Loxum Road the order must be:

Davis Street → Elyard Place → Jammu Parade. Note that she "crosses" Davis Street and Elyard Place (not "passes"). The word "crosses" means she runs across those roads.

What about the other side of the road?

Before she gets to Davis Close, two streets have been "passed". They must be on the other side of the road and must be Prem Street (first – as it is closest to Jana's house) and Mittal Avenue second. Len Lane is after Davis Close, so it must be third. The last road on this side must be Wurri Wurri Road, as it is the first on that is on her left as she returns. Hence Roselely Road must be between Wurri Wurri Road and Len Lane.

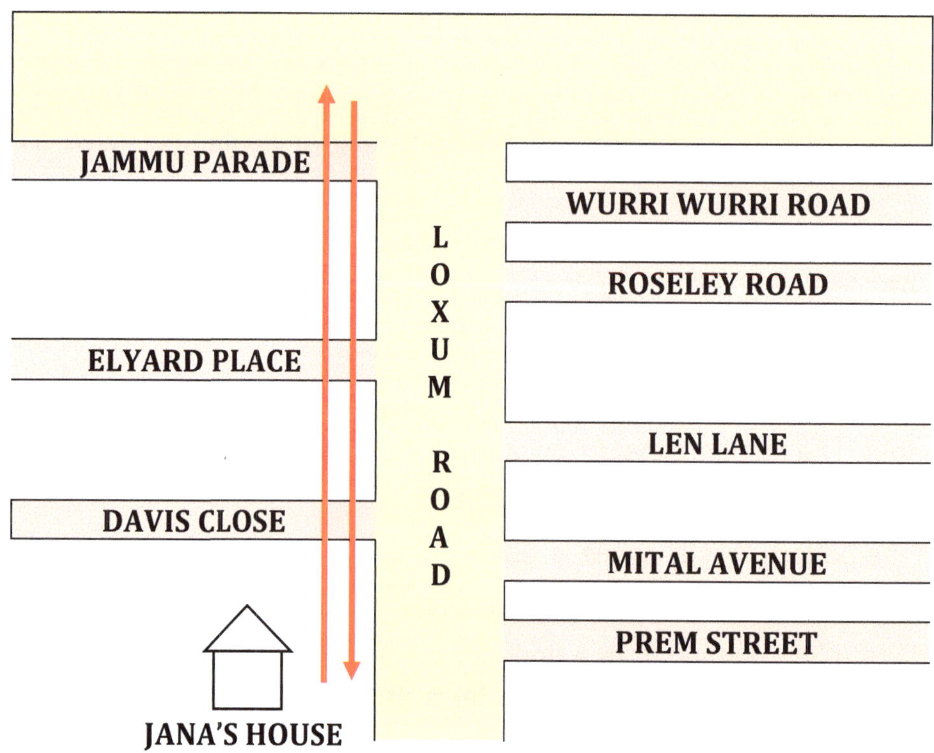

Question 33

B

The completed picture is shown below. The repeating pattern is shown in white.

Question 34

B

The situation here seems to suggest that the cause of Alisa's forgetfulness is low Omega-3 fatty levels. However, this suggestion has not been verified – it is implied only. Inductive reasoning could conclude that A is correct however, there is no suggestion that fish oil improves memory – this is also implied. Thus, A can be ruled out.

C is incorrect because, again, the cause of alias's forgetfulness is not known.

D cannot be concluded though it may be possible.

B is correct as the cause of Alisa's forgetfulness is unknown.

Question 35

C

If Roberta worked all day on Saturday and Sunday (weekend days), as in A, then she would get extra pay hence this does explain a reason. If Roberta worked additional hours she would also get extra pay hence B can explain her extra pay. If Roberta replaced the supervisor, she would be on increased pay so this also explains her additional income.

However, C does not explain why Roberta received extra income, as being asked to work overtime is not the same as working overtime. Roberta may have declined. Hence, C is correct.

Question 36

D

The pieces fit together as shown here.

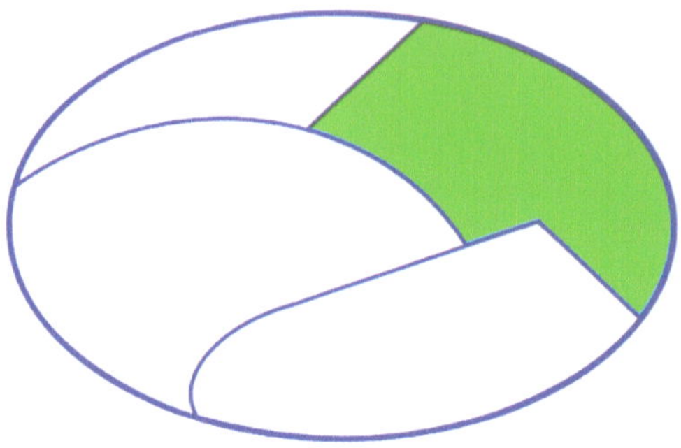

Answers

Question 37

B

What we know

Jane knows that on the ground, when she jumps up as high as she can, it takes her 0.5 seconds to land. Jane steps into a lift and presses the button to another floor.

Solution

Consider Jane and the lift as separate things. Taking each of the answers in order:

If Jane jumps up as high as she can the instant the lift moves up the lift will rise up and she will have less distance to fall to touch the lift floor. So, A is true.

Similarly with C: If Jane jumps up as high as she can the instant the lift moves down, she will be in the air for more than 0.5 seconds because the floor of the lift will be moving away from her as she lands.

Also with D: If Jane jumps up as high as she can the moment the lift is slowing down as it approaches an upper floor, she will be in the air for longer than 0.5 seconds because she will be moving upwards faster than the floor of the lift is slowing.

If Jane jumps up as high as she can as the lift moves downwards at constant speed, she will be in the air for more than 0.5 seconds. This cannot be true as a lift moving at a steady or constant speed is similar to it being still. Hence, she should be in the air for 0.5 seconds – not more or less.

Question 38

C

The trend is that Sydney's stock markets are conditional on movements in New York stock markets – as "if → then" statements are used.

Consequently, the "if → then" relationship must be understood:

1. Sydney stock markets follow the New York stock markets
2. There is a time difference of more than one day (but less than 2 days) We can deduce that trading doesn't happen on a weekend.

Hence, what happens on Wednesday in New York will not affect Sydney until Friday. Hence the only correct conclusion is C.

Question 39

A

310 people were to identify their favourite form of drink. The results are shown in the table below.

Bottled Water	51	Chai Tea	53
Flat White Coffee	160	Green Tea	46

Only these four drinks were chosen. The information was entered into a spreadsheet in order to construct a pie chart. However, some of the data was incorrectly entered. Consequently, this was the pie chart that appeared on the screen.

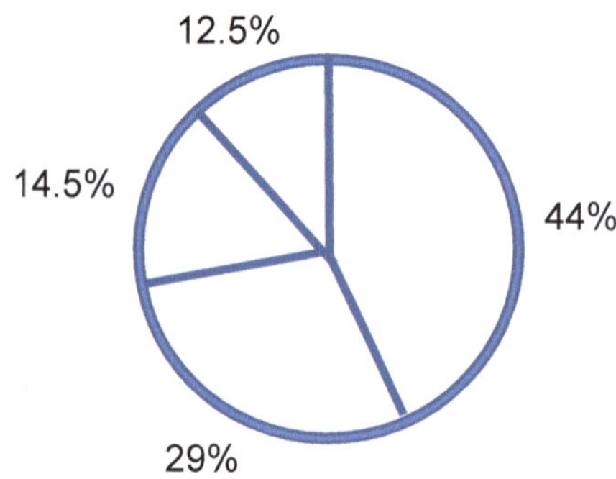

Solution

The data for each option and the proportions are shown in the table below:

	Unadulterated data (%)	Flat White recorded as 116	Green Tea recorded as 64	Bottled Water recorded as 105	Chai Tea recorded as 35
Flat White	160/310 = 52%	116/266 = 44%	160/328 = 49%	160/364 = 44%	160/292 = 55%
Chai Tea	53/310 = 17%	53/266 = 20%	53/328 = 16%	53/364 = 14.5%	35/292 = 12%
Bottled Water	51/310 = 16.5%	51/266 = 19%	51/328 = 15.5%	105/364 = 29%	51/292 = 17.5%
Green Tea	46/310 = 15%	46/266 = 17%	64/328 = 19.5%	46/364 = 12.5%	46/292 = 16%
Total	**100%**	**100%**	**100%**	**100%**	**100%**

Question 40

A

B is not an appropriate hypothesis as the lift as the lift continues up from the 4th Floor to the 7th Floor without anyone in the lift pressing the 7th Floor button. C does not really make sense as it depends on when and where a person catches the lift. The person on the 4th as the lift goes down experiences the lift going down. If they stay on the lift then after it goes down it will go up.

D may be possible, but is outside of the experience Mohsin had. Mohsin does not know whether the lift came from above him downwards or below him upwards.

A is correct as Mohsin experiences the lift travelling upwards to a person on a higher floor wanting to come down despite him pressing to a lower floor. This experience is repeated by what he observes when he returns to the 2nd Floor. Here a person presses the 3rd Floor button but the lift continues downwards to the Ground Floor.

Question 41

C

There are a minimum of 20 small cubes in the figure, all of which are visible. The maximum is 29 (9 in the back row, then 5 (with 1 visible), then 8 (all visible) + 7).

Question 42

C

A is incorrect as a placebo is not just "fake medicine." It is meant to be given under circumstances where the patient believes they are taking real, effective medicine. B is also incorrect as though half of the people in the experiment did recover in 7 days, it does not mean that all people will recover in twice the time. The medicine may only be effective for about 50% of people, for example. The experiment assesses the effect of a placebo – not how people think (without taking anything), hence D must be incorrect.

C is correct as it is possible to validly conclude that people using a placebo do heal faster than those who do not use any medicine or any placebo (ie they do nothing)

Question 43

B

Look closely at the tile pattern presented below and look at the red arrows.

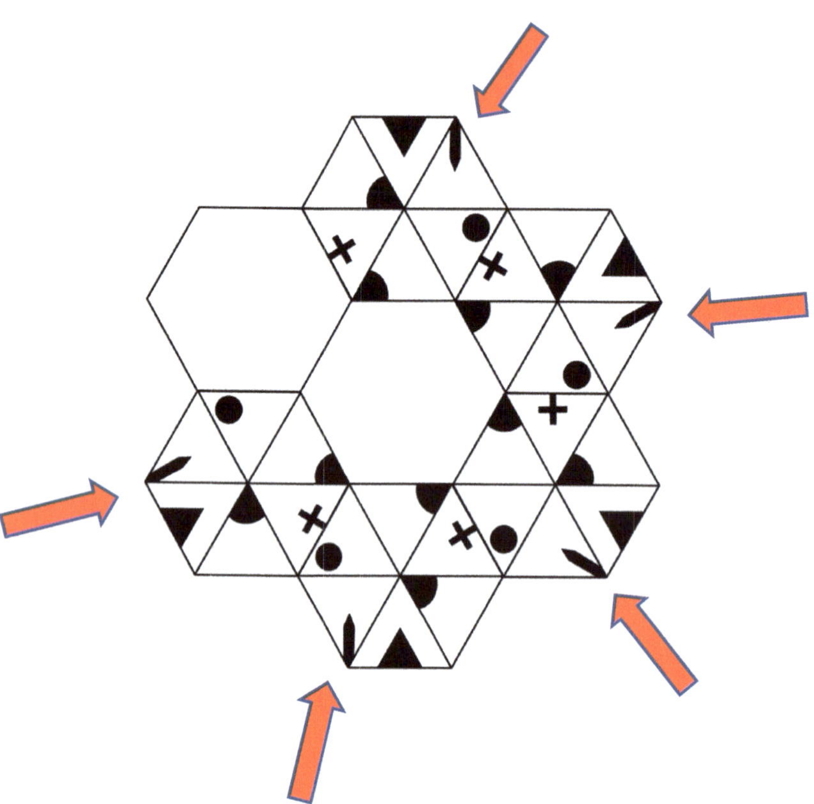

The panel that should replace the ? is B following the anticlockwise rotation.

B.

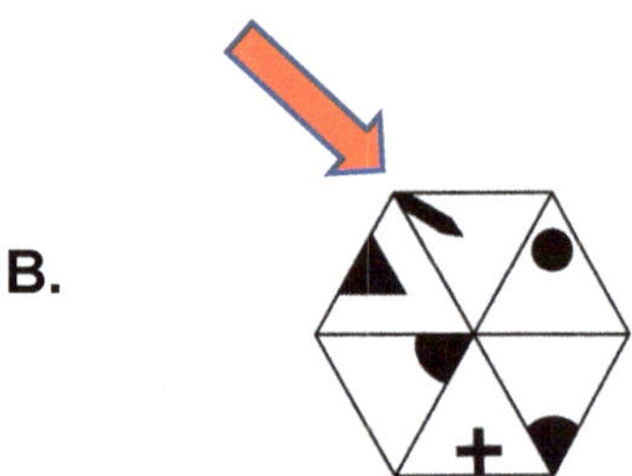

Question 44

D

The verbs need to be placed in order of levels. In this case the order is called "levels of cognition" or thinking.

Taking the sentences in order:

In order to analyse you need to be able to explain.

Hence analyse is above explain.

In order to describe you need to be able to recall.

Hence describe is above recall.

The <u>next three sentences are linked</u>:

In order to evaluate you need to be able to show the link between cause and effect. Evaluate means to make a judgment based on criteria. Explain means to show the link between cause and effect.

Evaluate (make a judgment based on criteria) is above explain (show the link between cause and effect).

These sentences are linked:

Describe means to provide the characteristics and features of something. If you can show the link between cause and effect, then you can also provide the characteristics and features of something.

Explain (show the link between cause and effect) is above describe (provide the characteristics and features of things).

Hence the ***KNOWN*** order is: Evaluate → Explain → Describe → Recall.

What is not known is whether Analyse is above Evaluate or below it, but we do know it is above Explain.

Since Dani is able to analyse things well, then Dani must be able to Explain (show the link between cause and effect), Describe (provide the characteristics and features of things) and Recall. Hence A, B and C are correct. We do not know whether Dani can Evaluate hence D must not necessarily be true.

Question 45

C

Look closely at the pattern in the stained-glass window shown below and the completed pattern.

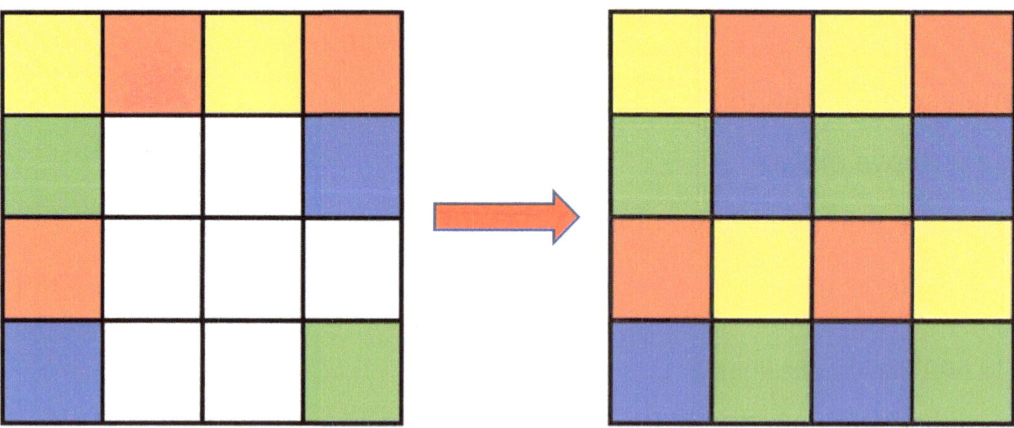

Which of the following arrangements completes the pattern on the stained-glass?

C This can be seen by rotating the stained-glass clockwise by 90 degrees.

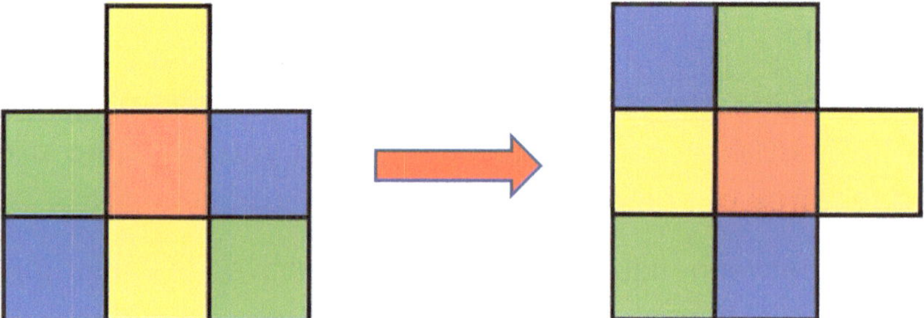

Alternatively, identify that as the left column has four different colours then the right column might also have four different colours. Rotating the pieces to fit the puzzle leaves C as the only piece to allow the pieces in the right column to be different. Selecting that piece then satisfies the 2nd and 3rd rows to satisfy the condition that rows will have two alternating colours – Row 1: yellow, red, yellow, red Row 2: green, blue, green, blue Row 3: red, yellow, red, yellow and Row 4: blue. green, blue, green.

Question 46

C

The completed pattern is as follows:

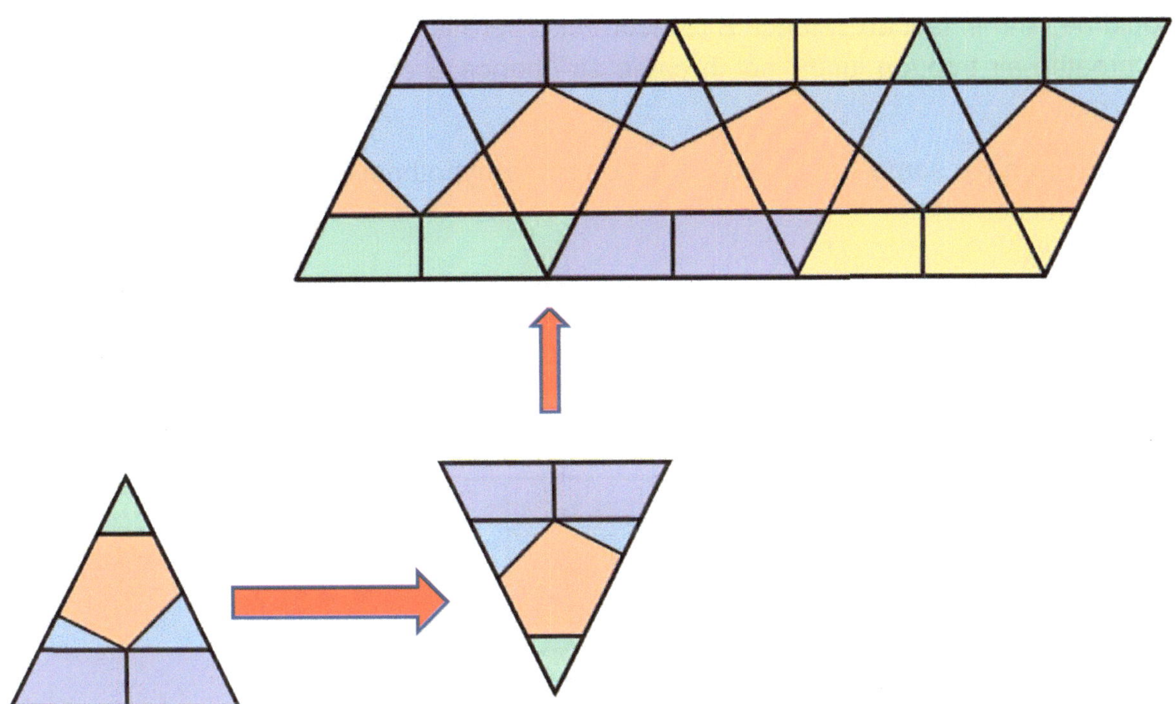

It can be seen that the black lines join and the shape needs to be rotated to give the correct answer.

Question 47

A

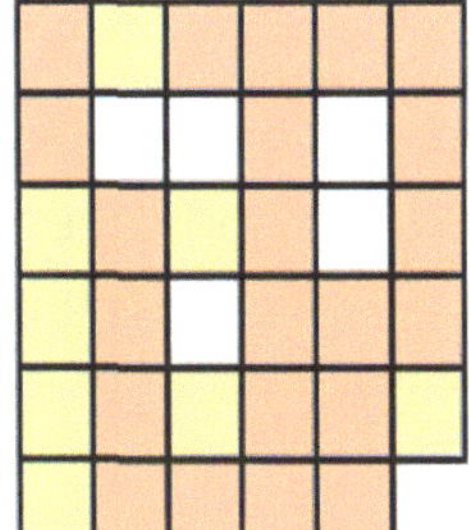

Question 48

D

Since birds lay eggs they cannot be mammals so A must be incorrect. Since mammals MOSTLY are diphyodonts we cannot hypothesise that they are not mammals - as they could be, and in fact are! Hence B is incorrect. There is nothing to support C as the fact is 'breathe air through lungs' not 'breathe air', hence C cannot be hypothesised and is incorrect.

Whales do have some hair and so it is correct to hypothesise that they are mammals, hence D is correct.

Question 49

B

The astute eye will see the following: the yellow shape is moving clockwise through the triangle as is the green shape. This is shown with red arrows below:

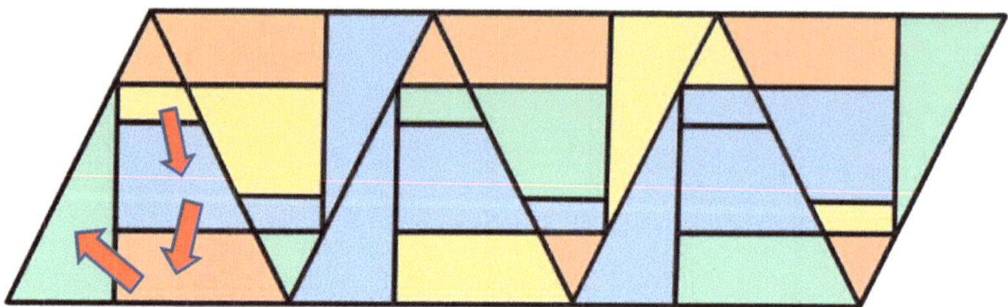

Look carefully: the yellow colour is moving between the different shapes. This means that the missing shape must have a yellow triangle. The same can be seen for the green shape as well, but moving in the reverse direction. Hence the answer is B. However, the shape needs to be rotated to make it fit.

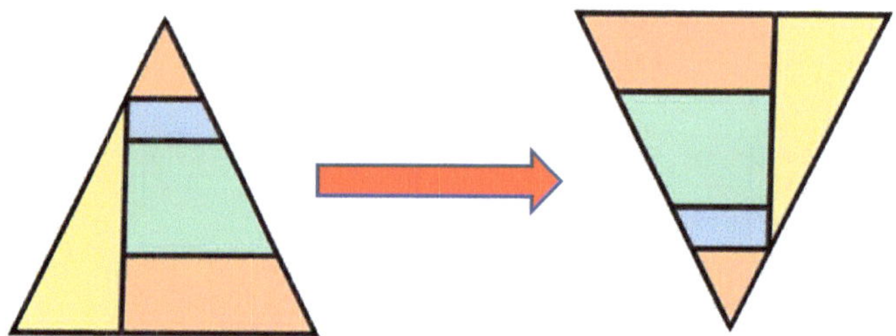

Question 50

A

We do not know whether Kepler's tears are from the onion vapours or from being deeply upset. Hence, we cannot be certain that B is correct so it must be ruled out. This also rules out C (for the same reason). D is possible but not certain – the use of the word "will" makes this option incorrect.

A is correct as Kepler's tears would have been caused by either the onion vapours, or the emotions he felt (or both). Emotional tears have more hormones than other tears.

Question 51

A

The number of wheels on the trucks is 4 × 6 = 24. Hence the number of wheels remaining for the cars and motorbikes is 112.

This means that the sum of the wheels on the 33 other vehicles is 112.

All these other vehicles have at least two wheels.

33 × 2 = 66 wheels.

112 – 66 = 46 wheels that must be on cars.

Since two wheels on these cars have already been counted, then each of the remaining cars needs two wheels counted. This means there are 46 ÷ 2 = 23 cars.

Hence, we know there are 4 trucks with 24 wheels.

23 cars with 23 × 4 wheels = 92 wheels.

These together account for 116 wheels.

Consequently, there must be 10 motorbikes with 20 wheels in total.

Question 52

D

This can be analysed using a Venn Diagram as shown below.

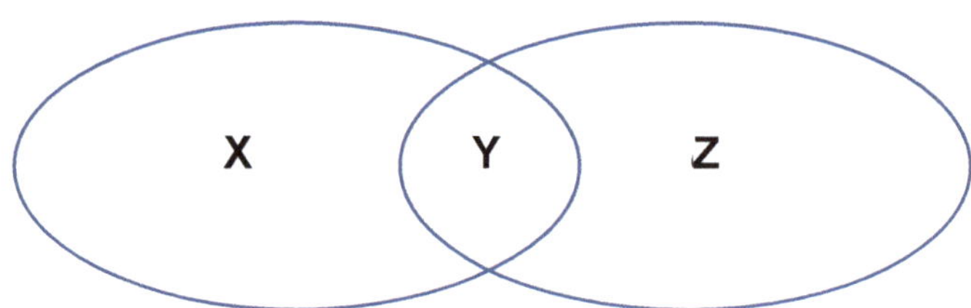

Let X = Children who ONLY wear short-sleeved shirts
Let Y = Children who wear BOTH a short-sleeved shirt and hat
Let Z = Children who ONLY wear a hat

We know that:

X + Y = 148
Y + Z = 170

X + Y + Z = 255 – 43 = 212

Since X + Y = 148, and X + Y + Z = 212 then this can be rewritten as: 148 + Z = 212

So, Z = 64

Hence Y = 106 and X must be 42.

As Z = 64 the number of children who wear hats but not a long sleeve shirt is 64.

Answers

Question 53

B

This can be analysed using a Venn Diagram as shown below.

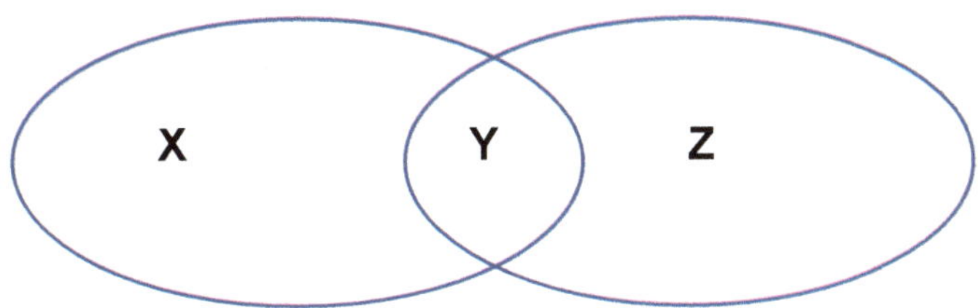

Let X = Sheep shorn in the period 1 Jan to 31 March
Let Y = Sheep shorn in April
Let Z = Sheep shorn in May and June

We know that:

X + Y = 65
Y + Z = 45

x + Y + Z = 80

Since X + Y = 65, and X + Y + Z = 80 then this can be rewritten as: 65 + Z = 80

So, Z = 15

Hence Y = 30 and X must be 35.

So, 30 sheep are shorn in April as shown in B.

Use the following information to do Question 54 and 55.

Nolan gets his salary paid on Thursday every fortnight. This year he gets paid three salary payments in two different months. This happens first in April. Nolan's first April pay comes arrives on the first day of the month.

Question 54

B

There are three Thursday fortnights that occur TWICE each year in any given year. In this instance his first Thursday pay is on the April 1. So, his second pay is on the 15th and the third is on 29th April.

In May his pays are on Thursday the 6th and Thursday 20th.

In June his pays are on Thursday 3rd and Thursday 17th.

In July his pays are on July 1st, 15th and 29th. Hence the answer is B.

Question 55

C

2024 is a leap year with January commencing on a Monday. In which months would Nolan get 3 pays?

If January 1st is a Monday in 2024, then Nolan will get his first January pay on January 4th. His second will be on January 18th and his next pay will be on February 1st. Then it will be Feb 15th and Feb 29th. If you follow this pattern you will find that the next month with three pay Thursdays is August. You can see this on the calendar below.

2024

January

Su	M	Tu	W	Th	F	Sa
	1	2	3	4	5	6
7	8	9	10	11	12	13
14	15	16	17	18	19	20
21	22	23	24	25	26	27
28	29	30	31			

February

Su	M	Tu	W	Th	F	Sa
				1	2	3
4	5	6	7	8	9	10
11	12	13	14	15	16	17
18	19	20	21	22	23	24
25	26	27	28	29		

March

Su	M	Tu	W	Th	F	Sa
					1	2
3	4	5	6	7	8	9
10	11	12	13	14	15	16
17	18	19	20	21	22	23
24	25	26	27	28	29	30
31						

April

Su	M	Tu	W	Th	F	Sa
	1	2	3	4	5	6
7	8	9	10	11	12	13
14	15	16	17	18	19	20
21	22	23	24	25	26	27
28	29	30				

May

Su	M	Tu	W	Th	F	Sa
			1	2	3	4
5	6	7	8	9	10	11
12	13	14	15	16	17	18
19	20	21	22	23	24	25
26	27	28	29	30	31	

June

Su	M	Tu	W	Th	F	Sa
						1
2	3	4	5	6	7	8
9	10	11	12	13	14	15
16	17	18	19	20	21	22
23	24	25	26	27	28	29
30						

July

Su	M	Tu	W	Th	F	Sa
	1	2	3	4	5	6
7	8	9	10	11	12	13
14	15	16	17	18	19	20
21	22	23	24	25	26	27
28	29	30	31			

August

Su	M	Tu	W	Th	F	Sa
				1	2	3
4	5	6	7	8	9	10
11	12	13	14	15	16	17
18	19	20	21	22	23	24
25	26	27	28	29	30	31

September

Su	M	Tu	W	Th	F	Sa
1	2	3	4	5	6	7
8	9	10	11	12	13	14
15	16	17	18	19	20	21
22	23	24	25	26	27	28
29	30					

October

Su	M	Tu	W	Th	F	Sa
		1	2	3	4	5
6	7	8	9	10	11	12
13	14	15	16	17	18	19
20	21	22	23	24	25	26
27	28	29	30	31		

November

Su	M	Tu	W	Th	F	Sa
					1	2
3	4	5	6	7	8	9
10	11	12	13	14	15	16
17	18	19	20	21	22	23
24	25	26	27	28	29	30

December

Su	M	Tu	W	Th	F	Sa
1	2	3	4	5	6	7
8	9	10	11	12	13	14
15	16	17	18	19	20	21
22	23	24	25	26	27	28
29	30	31				

Question 56

B

Whilst there has been an announcement, there is nothing to suggest there is a lockdown. Hence, we cannot be sure that Anya is correct.

Monya words, "Maybe..." indicate a possibility and, though unlikely, she may be correct. Hence B is correct.

Question 57

A

Looking closely at the diagram we can see the direction of the wind flow. This is shown in **red** below.

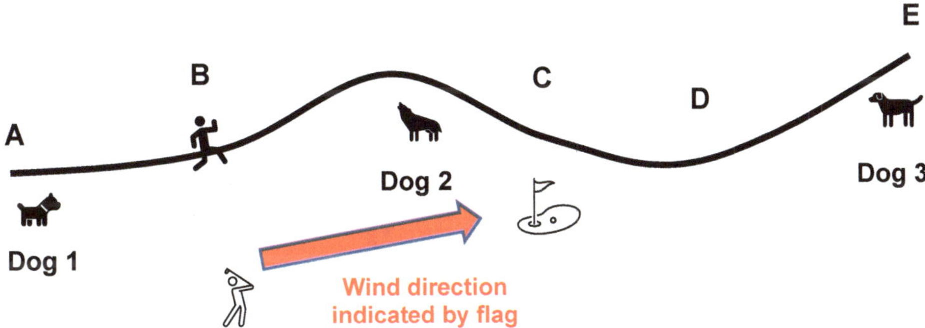

Since Dog 1 can see Djarko we cannot conclude this, and it is incorrect. C must be incorrect as the dogs only bark when he is in particular positions. Futhermore, as Dog 1 must hear him, since he passes it, we cannot conclude a response to sound. Given the wind direction and the barking occurring both there and back on Djarko's journey, A must be correct.

Question 58

D

A is true as all reptiles are cold blooded – since there are no reptiles that are not cold blooded. B is also true as vertebrate fish fall within the within the category of cold blooded animals. This is also true of C

D is incorrect as there may be other animals that also breathe oxygen – such as mammals – and hence in "a group" there can be animals that are neither reptiles not vertebrate fish.

Question 59

B

All of the answers seem plausible! However, not all are correct ☺ The evidence shows that the children seem to be unable to perceive or comprehend the danger they face if Mohsin runs on the line he is running. This means A is a reasonable hypothesis. The evidence suggests that C is also correct as in each case a child did not take evasive action or cognise a threat. D appears to be a rational possibility.

B is incorrect as we do not know who the adults are with the children. They could be older siblings, uncles or carers. Hence this is not a correct hypothesis.

Question 60

A

Look closely at the pattern below. The red shows the clockwise rotation of the triangle. You can see this by looking at the rectangle shape. This is a rotation that would be mirrored in the other two panels.

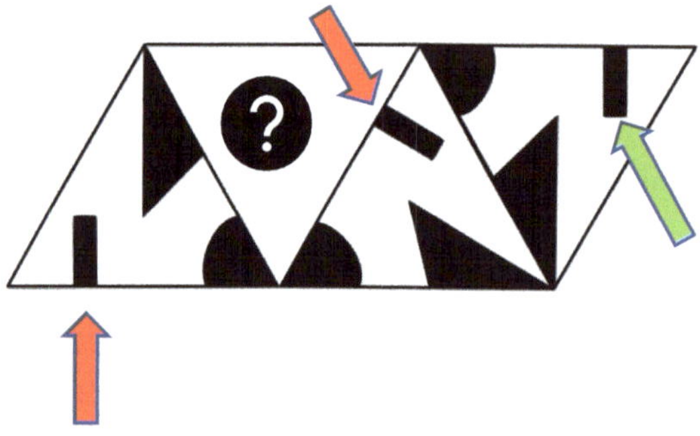

C is not possible because the corners are incorrect. This is true of D as well. Hence the options are A and B only. A must be correct as when rotated it will be in the correct position on the top right side.

A. 

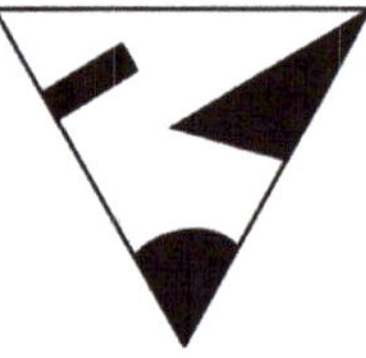

B.

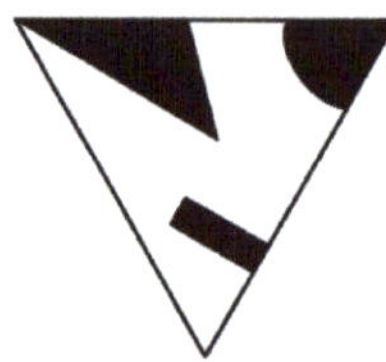

C.

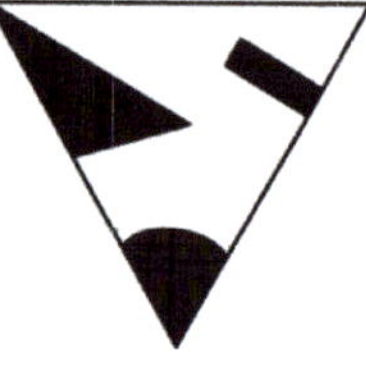

D.

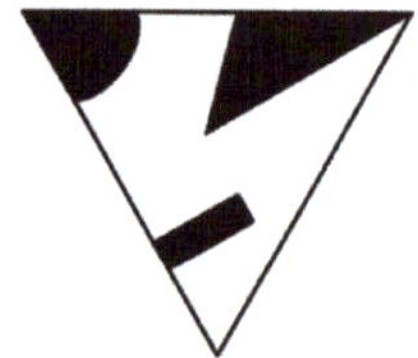

Critical Thinking Skills

FOR SELECTIVE SCHOOL TESTS, OPPORTUNITY CLASS TEST AND PROBLEM SOLVING

Use pencil when filling out this sheet

Fill in the circle correctly			
●	(B)	(C)	(D)

If you make a mistake neatly cross it out and circle the correct response			
⊗	●	(C)	(D)

MULTIPLE CHOICE ANSWER SHEET

1	(A)	(B)	(C)	(D)	31	(A)	(B)	(C)	(D)
2	(A)	(B)	(C)	(D)	32	(A)	(B)	(C)	(D)
3	(A)	(B)	(C)	(D)	33	(A)	(B)	(C)	(D)
4	(A)	(B)	(C)	(D)	34	(A)	(B)	(C)	(D)
5	(A)	(B)	(C)	(D)	35	(A)	(B)	(C)	(D)
6	(A)	(B)	(C)	(D)	36	(A)	(B)	(C)	(D)
7	(A)	(B)	(C)	(D)	37	(A)	(B)	(C)	(D)
8	(A)	(B)	(C)	(D)	38	(A)	(B)	(C)	(D)
9	(A)	(B)	(C)	(D)	39	(A)	(B)	(C)	(D)
10	(A)	(B)	(C)	(D)	40	(A)	(B)	(C)	(D)
11	(A)	(B)	(C)	(D)	41	(A)	(B)	(C)	(D)
12	(A)	(B)	(C)	(D)	42	(A)	(B)	(C)	(D)
13	(A)	(B)	(C)	(D)	43	(A)	(B)	(C)	(D)
14	(A)	(B)	(C)	(D)	44	(A)	(B)	(C)	(D)
15	(A)	(B)	(C)	(D)	45	(A)	(B)	(C)	(D)
16	(A)	(B)	(C)	(D)	46	(A)	(B)	(C)	(D)
17	(A)	(B)	(C)	(D)	47	(A)	(B)	(C)	(D)
18	(A)	(B)	(C)	(D)	48	(A)	(B)	(C)	(D)
19	(A)	(B)	(C)	(D)	49	(A)	(B)	(C)	(D)
20	(A)	(B)	(C)	(D)	50	(A)	(B)	(C)	(D)
21	(A)	(B)	(C)	(D)	51	(A)	(B)	(C)	(D)
22	(A)	(B)	(C)	(D)	52	(A)	(B)	(C)	(D)
23	(A)	(B)	(C)	(D)	53	(A)	(B)	(C)	(D)
24	(A)	(B)	(C)	(D)	54	(A)	(B)	(C)	(D)
25	(A)	(B)	(C)	(D)	55	(A)	(B)	(C)	(D)
26	(A)	(B)	(C)	(D)	56	(A)	(B)	(C)	(D)
27	(A)	(B)	(C)	(D)	57	(A)	(B)	(C)	(D)
28	(A)	(B)	(C)	(D)	58	(A)	(B)	(C)	(D)
29	(A)	(B)	(C)	(D)	59	(A)	(B)	(C)	(D)
30	(A)	(B)	(C)	(D)	60	(A)	(B)	(C)	(D)

Critical Thinking Skills

FOR SELECTIVE SCHOOL TESTS, OPPORTUNITY CLASS TEST AND PROBLEM SOLVING

Use pencil when filling out this sheet

Fill in the circle correctly			
●	B	C	D

If you make a mistake neatly cross it out and circle the correct response

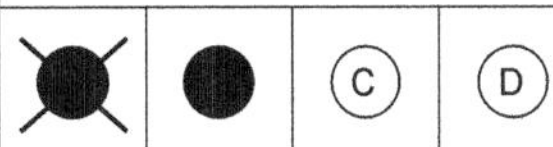

MULTIPLE CHOICE ANSWER SHEET

1	A	B	C	D	31	A	B	C	D
2	A	B	C	D	32	A	B	C	D
3	A	B	C	D	33	A	B	C	D
4	A	B	C	D	34	A	B	C	D
5	A	B	C	D	35	A	B	C	D
6	A	B	C	D	36	A	B	C	D
7	A	B	C	D	37	A	B	C	D
8	A	B	C	D	38	A	B	C	D
9	A	B	C	D	39	A	B	C	D
10	A	B	C	D	40	A	B	C	D
11	A	B	C	D	41	A	B	C	D
12	A	B	C	D	42	A	B	C	D
13	A	B	C	D	43	A	B	C	D
14	A	B	C	D	44	A	B	C	D
15	A	B	C	D	45	A	B	C	D
16	A	B	C	D	46	A	B	C	D
17	A	B	C	D	47	A	B	C	D
18	A	B	C	D	48	A	B	C	D
19	A	B	C	D	49	A	B	C	D
20	A	B	C	D	50	A	B	C	D
21	A	B	C	D	51	A	B	C	D
22	A	B	C	D	52	A	B	C	D
23	A	B	C	D	53	A	B	C	D
24	A	B	C	D	54	A	B	C	D
25	A	B	C	D	55	A	B	C	D
26	A	B	C	D	56	A	B	C	D
27	A	B	C	D	57	A	B	C	D
28	A	B	C	D	58	A	B	C	D
29	A	B	C	D	59	A	B	C	D
30	A	B	C	D	60	A	B	C	D

Critical Thinking Skills

FOR SELECTIVE SCHOOL TESTS, OPPORTUNITY CLASS TEST AND PROBLEM SOLVING

Use pencil when filling out this sheet

Fill in the circle correctly			
●	B	C	D

If you make a mistake neatly cross it out and circle the correct response			
✗	●	C	D

MULTIPLE CHOICE ANSWER SHEET

1	A	B	C	D	31	A	B	C	D
2	A	B	C	D	32	A	B	C	D
3	A	B	C	D	33	A	B	C	D
4	A	B	C	D	34	A	B	C	D
5	A	B	C	D	35	A	B	C	D
6	A	B	C	D	36	A	B	C	D
7	A	B	C	D	37	A	B	C	D
8	A	B	C	D	38	A	B	C	D
9	A	B	C	D	39	A	B	C	D
10	A	B	C	D	40	A	B	C	D
11	A	B	C	D	41	A	B	C	D
12	A	B	C	D	42	A	B	C	D
13	A	B	C	D	43	A	B	C	D
14	A	B	C	D	44	A	B	C	D
15	A	B	C	D	45	A	B	C	D
16	A	B	C	D	46	A	B	C	D
17	A	B	C	D	47	A	B	C	D
18	A	B	C	D	48	A	B	C	D
19	A	B	C	D	49	A	B	C	D
20	A	B	C	D	50	A	B	C	D
21	A	B	C	D	51	A	B	C	D
22	A	B	C	D	52	A	B	C	D
23	A	B	C	D	53	A	B	C	D
24	A	B	C	D	54	A	B	C	D
25	A	B	C	D	55	A	B	C	D
26	A	B	C	D	56	A	B	C	D
27	A	B	C	D	57	A	B	C	D
28	A	B	C	D	58	A	B	C	D
29	A	B	C	D	59	A	B	C	D
30	A	B	C	D	60	A	B	C	D